OVERTHINKING IS NOT THE SOLUTION: FOR TEENS

The Ultimate Guide to Discover How to Overcome Anxiety and Depression, Develop Your Self-Confidence and Live Fearlessly with Mindfulness

Robert J. Charles

Table of Contents

WANT TO OVERCOME OVERTHINKING and MANAGE DIFFICULT PEOPLE?

These **4 FREE** offers are perfect for you: 2 eBooks + 2 audiobooks.

In these 2 eBooks + 2 audiobooks, YOU will discover:

- The three different forms of overthinking and how to spot them.
- How ruminating and worrying can damage your social life.
- The types of toxic people and how to escape their web of crises.
- How to discover if you are a highly sensitive person and ways to deal with that.

If you want to finally stop overthinking and being manipulated by others...

Claim these 4 **FREE Offers. SCAN** this QR code with Your Camera:

SECOND BONUS
How to Face Any Challenge with Confidence
Download these **FREE 30 BIBLICAL PROMISES** to discover some powerful promises for **YOU**.

At some point, everyone on this Earth faces a tough challenge. Help is on the way! God has your back. His Word will empower you to face any trial or tribulation. These 30 promises from God will give you the strength and resilience you need to move forward.

To get your **FREE** 30 BIBLICAL PROMISES TO OVERCOME ANY CHALLENGE, **SCAN this QR code with Your Camera:**

INTRODUCTION

Wow! It must have taken a lot to decide to give this book a shot. I mean…there are so many books out there that probably haven't given you the raw, consistent, and helpful information that you've spent all your teenage years looking for. I get that this might have been a stressful journey.

But you're here, yo! I'm excited because you've made my work easier by showing up. It's commendable that you're here because many of your friends will never decide to pick up a helpful book even though they're dealing with just about the same problems as you.

So, overthinking, yeah? Gosh, that stuff used to bother me like crazy. It's funny because it doesn't go away with adulthood. Did someone lie to you that it will? Because it won't. You can experience the trouble, pain, and confusion of thinking too much even as a full-grown adult man or woman.

If you are able to attack overthinking early in your teenage years, that's fantastic, because the longer you let that damn thing linger, the more likely it will become a trojan horse that destroys many things you attempt to build later in life.

What other damage can overthinking do to you? We'll dive into those things fully in the book, yeah, but just to give you an idea, let me mention a few quickly.

First, overthinking can hinder your self-confidence. In fact, it works the other way around, too; low self-confidence has been found as a common cause of overthinking. These two mind-boggling brats (overthinking and low self-confidence) can simply bounce energy off each other and get you caught in a vicious cycle as overthinking translates to low self-confidence and vice versa. In the second part of this book, we explore this in depth to help you escape this cycle completely.

Overthinking can also be the cancer that kills your dreams. If you engage in it, you'll just think and think and think the dreams away till you've deadened the entire excitement, thrill, or even the possibility of ever going for those dreams.

I once met someone who had always wanted to go skydiving, but she'd thought about it so much that all the possible ways things could go wrong had been displayed in her mind like a movie, over and over again. She had developed a tendency to overthink and to be fearful as a teenager. Now she's currently over thirty years old and still hasn't done it, and she doesn't know if she'll ever do it. But that's a kinda mild example because it's just skydiving, right?

What about this teenager, Cora, who needed a major surgery but took days thinking about whether or not to do it because she was working out all the possible scenarios that could go wrong? In fact, her fears were even stressful for me to listen to when she voiced them. I had to shut down my mind at some point. I knew I couldn't take it anymore when she began to discuss the possibility of the anesthesiologist overdosing her and then abusing her while she was passed out.

It's true that a million and one things can go wrong in life. It's also true that things don't always go as expected. But maybe what's most crucial is to remember how powerful our imaginations are; they can cheer us on or break us down. Even as a teenager, you're not exempt from taking responsibility for your thinking patterns starting right now.

Overthinking will complicate simple life stuff for you. You're interested in getting a pet? It sounds like a simple decision; all you need to do is…well, go get the pet. But for an overthinker, it's not quite so straightforward. There's an infinite amount of considering the kind of pet you want, then the place to get it, then the endless considerations of how you're going to feed and care for the pet.

Now, don't get me wrong. It's important to be rational, whether you're a teenager or an adult. In fact, I'm a huge fan of carefully considering one's decisions before taking them instead of just jumping at what seems to be the next cool thing to do. But contrary to what you may think, reality actually dims in the face of overthinking.

Where most of us have a problem is in finding the delicate balance.

It's possible. Personally, I've researched and practiced long enough to see that it's possible. I've tried all the principles discussed in this book myself, and I can tell you that it's possible to avoid overthinking without throwing your decisions into the hands of impulse. It's possible to be rational without going through rounds and rounds of complicated self-debate and second-guessing.

This book promises you a thorough understanding of overthinking. I'll also be discussing this sensitive topic in light of the Scriptures to give you a new perspective. The book will walk you through several biblical and contemporary stories, with examples and reasons why you need to stop believing that it is impossible to control your thoughts. My aim is to help you develop self-confidence and overcome anxiety, depression, or other underlying conditions that might make overthinking worse. Because whether overthinking leads to depression and anxiety or having depression makes you overthink, both can be exhausting. You will never live your best life until you learn to let certain things roll off your mind and move on.

Are you ready for this?

As you join me on this exciting journey, take a picture now; then take another picture when we're done with the book and let me know the difference you see, because I am very optimistic that you will emerge a changed person.

Part 1

Understanding Your Overthinking Issues

They say that one of the best ways to live is to focus on controlling what you can and leave aside what you can't control. I like that thought. I mean, what's the point of bothering about whether or not rain will fall on a particular day? Nah, just get an umbrella and have a raincoat handy. It's beyond our control to dictate to the Master of the universe how the weather is run.

A problem occurs, however, when people sometimes mix up what they can control and what they can't. If you continuously try to control what you can't, you'll give yourself unnecessary stress and anxiety. On the other hand, if you relinquish power and refuse to control what you should, you'll also have a problem. For example, your thought-controlling ability is one of those that you shouldn't ever consider relinquishing, because it's everything.

"For as he thinketh in his heart, so is he…"

—Proverbs 23:7

Your thinking patterns reveal your true nature. If you tend to let toxic thoughts fly around in your head, you will eventually start acting like your thoughts. If anger, sadness, and depression have your mind all warped, there's just no telling what might happen because thoughts tell a lot about a person's tendencies.

Understanding your overthinking issues is a very crucial step in getting your thoughts on track. That's what this part is based on, and I strongly believe that you're going to have a lot of strengthening revelation as you go through this part.

CHAPTER ONE

"Even though I walk through the darkest valley, I will fear no evil, for you are with me; your rod and your staff, they comfort me."

—Psalm 23:4

HELP! MY MIND WON'T REST

Imagine it's your first day at a new school after your family had to move because your dad got a promotion. As happy as everyone is because of the promotion and career progress, it doesn't stop you from sulking because it's the third time you're changing towns in two years.

You moved to the city, away from your quiet neighborhood where everyone knew everyone and it didn't take a lot to get to know new people because the synergy there was so lit. You had a good life at that small-town school and were quite popular. But now you're in a fast-growing, busy city where nobody cares about you, and you have to either look out for yourself or get lost in the crowd.

You walk into school on the first day. Your hair is short. Everyone starts whispering about how you look like a boy, how you look weird because you're not wearing makeup, and how your outfit looks like it was put together by a caveman. Of course, you are smiling and hoping to make new friends, but they already think you're weird and are waiting for you to make a mistake so they can laugh at you.

And boom! You do not disappoint them; you speak in class with a rather unpretentious accent, and everyone begins to laugh. You suck it up and continue to introduce yourself. Later on, the teacher asks a question; you dare to raise your hand, but give an unsatisfying answer. She asks for an alternative, and now you feel embarrassed because the other students are whispering loudly about you not being intelligent. You can't take it anymore, so you get up to use the bathroom. Moving quickly, you bump into a desk on your way out, get pushed by the desk owner, and hit the floor.

You get up quickly, hearing the kids laugh around you, and head for the door. But then the principal opens the door before you can reach it, so the door bumps against your head, and you fall to the ground again. You hear the laughter double in volume.

When you're finally at home and lying in bed, you start pondering what a terrible day you had. You can't stop thinking about it. That one bad day turns into a week, and one week into months, and you can hardly sleep at night because you're so anxious and stressed.

Okay, true, that was not your story, but you might be able to understand why this tenth grader would find it challenging to shut her mind down for a moment and rest. Why it would be almost impossible to stop thinking about her old town, and why she would be anxious and stressed and would keep having bad days.

The chaos that comes from overthinking doesn't get easier. It's like being scheduled for one piece of bad news after another without a break. It's like a bad day becoming a bad year and then a bad life if something is not done.

Does it really have to be this horrifying?

WHAT IS OVERTHINKING?

So what's the catch? Will overthinking just disappear because you want it to? Simple answer: no.

Overthinking is significantly associated with chronic pain. When a person is suffering, all they think about is how to stop suffering or make the pain less excruciating. But while overthinking is also associated with conditions like depression, anxiety, eating disorders, and sleep disorders, it's not necessarily a mental disorder. What is it then?

As the word suggests, it is simply excessive thinking: romanticizing or obsessing over a particular thought (usually a negative one). It involves picking out every tiny detail from a situation and trying to build those into false giant facts such that what was subtle and negligible becomes very obvious. But the overthinking doesn't even stop there.

Once the giant details have been built, they become a huge headache, and the overthinker has to quickly embark on a new journey to try to simplify them for more analysis. And the more they try to simplify them, the more stuck they get in their overthinking rut. Eventually, worry about unrealistic and adverse outcomes comes in and makes them feel anxious and stressed.

Thinking about something a few times does not make it overthinking just yet. If you had a bad day and start thinking about it, for example, it could be for different reasons; one reason could be to introspect and realize what to avoid next time to ensure a good day. Another reason could be because you feel terrible about something and need to make amends with a few decisions you made.

But it can be easy to slip into overthinking if you begin to turn the events of the day over and over in your mind aimlessly, just letting it get annoying, strenuous, and probably even guilt-inducing.

One person thinks about his mistake so he can avoid it and move on. The other person chooses to absorb every detail and begins to imagine adverse outcomes—outcomes that are yet to happen and may likely never happen. Person A is not an overthinker, but Person B definitely is one.

Like I said, thinking about things is not wrong in itself. It is, in fact, vital for decision-making. Our everyday routine demands we think about things ahead of time to enable us to make the right choices. Thinking ahead of a decision can help you avoid mistakes and serious errors. The real issue comes in when, because you're analyzing and charting your course (something that's supposed to be a good thing), you're only worrying and getting more and more indecisive about a decision.

SIGNS THAT YOU ARE OVERTHINKING

Thinking is a gift that I personally cherish. There are some things you don't want to wish on yourself, and one of those is not being able to think critically. I don't know what would happen if we couldn't think as humans. The truth is that in this crucial stage of life and development as teenagers, our thoughts can easily become our only cool companions when the going gets tough.

It's even sweeter when we can talk to ourselves as we think. Have you tried that talking to yourself thing? Oh, you should. It's cool. Just make sure you do it when you're alone so people don't misunderstand you more than they already have. But try it today.

So I count the ability to think as a cool, cool gift. Without it, many of us would be irrational and inconsiderate. We'd act on a whim and not care who got hurt. But thank goodness we can think! Thank goodness that even as a teenager, you're able to think carefully about your life—how it has gone, how it's going, and how it'll go. That's a beautiful thing.

But when it becomes a matter of overthinking? Nah, that needs to be attended to.

So what signs let you know for sure that you're overthinking? You see, it's easier to notice a problem in someone else's life than it is to notice it in yours. Just like other people would notice faster that you hadn't brushed your teeth in a week than you would, even though your nose is right above your mouth.

Yet before any changes can be effected, we must realize that something has broken that needs fixing. The purpose of sharing the signs of overthinking at this point is to enable you to come quickly to the realization of what you're battling with in order to begin to retrace your steps.

Relentless, fruitless muddling up

One sign of overthinking is that you seem to be running in circles about a particular decision, problem, mistake, or flaw. You thought about it yesterday; the exact conversation you overheard last month is still ringing in your head without any ideas to help you confront or act differently on what was said.

Now, you've forgotten about reasoning; those gossips don't know you overheard them, yet you're beginning to have insomnia. This is because studies have shown that overthinking makes it hard for you to fall asleep at night (Sanghvi & Nakhat, 2020).

Are you noticing that non-stop muddling of your mind that makes it seem like you don't exactly have any direction with your thoughts but just keep whirling and whirling around? Hello! You're overthinking.

Replays of your mistakes

An overthinker is bad at letting go of their personal mistakes and shortcomings. And if there's anyone who thinks they've got a lot of shortcomings, it's a teenager. You. Imagine the horror of constantly hating your imperfections and then overthinking based on that.

Nobody likes me because I'm not slim.

I'm not a cool rich kid, so I don't fit in.

I walk clumsily and that's why I bump into things.

Fancy thinking those same thoughts every single day until the flaws define you. With the tendency to overthink, magnifying your own imperfections is the order of the day.

Chronic second-guessing of self

When you're also constantly second-guessing yourself and your ability to make decisions, you're probably thinking too much. Is it too hard to decide not to attend a school function and then make peace with that decision? Will your mind ever rest about it, or will it keep reminding you of what you might have missed and how the decision to stay away was wrong even though you can't see *why* it's wrong? That's a serious issue with overthinking there.

Constant negativity and negative thoughts

There's a problem with overthinking if you can't stop imagining the worst. I have memories of negative thinking plaguing me when I was seventeen-ish. For whatever reason, I was afraid my mother would die. Every time she went out or took a trip, I would sit in my room, my head throbbing with the thoughts of getting that bad call that something had happened to her. Nothing ever happened to her, of course, but my head throbbed either way. How about waiting for exam results or hoping for some good news? Overthinking has its way of showing up just then to plague us.

Sleeping issues

Speaking of negative thoughts, sleeping issues kind of naturally follow that. When all you can do is lie there and think bad thoughts about everything, your body will bear the brunt and your mind won't shut down. Sleeping issues aren't cool; they make everything worse because then you have to worry about your body too, and the myriad of problems that come with not being able to sleep.

Never making a decision on time

You know it's overthinking when instead of looking to solve a problem, you are merely lodging the thought of it. When you're overthinking, you become indecisive. So, indecisiveness is another sign of overthinking and prevents you from actualizing simple decisions. Even when a decision is finally made, you likely second-guess it.

HOW OVERTHINKING SPIRALS INTO NEGATIVE THOUGHTS

There's an interesting explanation for how overthinking can quickly spiral into extremely bothersome negative thoughts.

A hormone called dopamine is a neurotransmitter in the brain that makes you feel all those warm and fuzzy good feelings. This dopamine is released when you feel good and happy with yourself. On the contrary, there's another one called cortisol, which is the neurotransmitter released when you are having a bad day or feeling sad (Leonard et al., 2018).

Cortisol flows more freely than dopamine to incite negative thoughts, which is why we often find it easier to hold on to negative feelings rather than positive ones. But this is where it gets interesting. The brain releases these neurotransmitters basically to warn us when there is a possible danger based on the activities around us. When cortisol is released even before an unfortunate incident happens, that's your brain trying to get you ready so you can either avoid the danger or manage the possibility of that danger happening.

For example, let's say you have two days to display your science project and are far behind. worrying about it actually makes your brain release cortisol to enable you to work harder to prepare for the presentation. That impulse to work harder comes from your brain painting pictures of possible consequences if you fail to meet the deadline—

embarrassment, the teacher's disapproval, shame, dropping grades, or whatever else—they all come rushing at you.

That is how negative thoughts come about and start to bother you. The brain might mean this to protect you and help you make your deadline, but you might not realize that and just go into panic mode, beginning to imagine the worst while feeling too paralyzed to do anything about it.

While riding the bus to school, a car screeching loudly beside the bus can cause your brain to quickly release cortisol to warn you of the danger of a car accident. When you forget to run some important errand, the same response may be elicited. All the while, even though there is no accident or mom screaming at you for forgetting to run the errands, your brain will still warn you so you can prevent those dangers from actually happening.

It gets even worse when we are in a toxic environment with people who say hurtful things, keep their distance, and avoid eye contact. In a situation like that, all our brain can release is cortisol…it's like alarm bells ringing from every direction.

You might be asking: What, then, is the point of releasing all those neurotransmitters when they'll just make you scared and stuck in one place?

If you don't realize that your brain is only trying to protect you by the signals it sends, you're going to focus too much on the imaginary scenarios running through your mind. In focusing on those, you'll let your thinking run so wild, you'll be shocked at what negative thoughts will rapidly overtake you.

THE PROBLEM WITH OVERTHINKING (NEGATIVE EFFECTS OF OVERTHINKING)

Overthinking never ends with itself. It is like a conduit pipe leading you somewhere, and the journey never ends until you hit the brakes and turn away. The problems with overthinking are numerous.

1. Procrastination

Procrastination is a terrible habit that can arise from overthinking. It involves persuading yourself to ignore the vital thing you must do and focusing on a trivial one instead.

It is the inability (or refusal actually) to motivate yourself to do what is crucial. Instead of doing what's required of you, you simply manufacture an excuse to convince yourself to do something else, something with zero value, like just staring at the wall thinking about nothing—or thinking about anything other than what's helpful.

An overthinker will likely procrastinate by worrying about a job that they'll never get around to doing. Inevitably, productivity arises from brainstorming, planning, and constructively thinking through the task at hand, but overthinking messes all those up and merely leads to inactivity.

Parkinson's Law states that "work expands to fill the time allotted for its completion" (McKay & Richard, 2022). I agree, but...sometimes that stuff isn't black and white, as you may have found out yourself at times when you had a deadline.

A procrastinator cannot complete an assignment given one month ago in two days, as Parkinson's Law suggests—no! The procrastinator cannot work under pressure. Pressure can cripple anyone, and it beats me why you'd want to work under pressure when you can spread out the work over days and still enjoy it.

Overthinking and procrastination work hand in hand to create a life of frustration. If you notice that you keep postponing important tasks till you eventually never do them or are "forced" to do a shoddy job under pressure, you're already experiencing the terrible effects of overthinking and you've got to do something about it pretty fast.

2. Sleeping issues

Now, sleeping issues might arise because the mind won't shut down and the inner voice won't stop talking. Overthinking trains your brain to stay alert at night because, since you've taught it to overthink events, it begins to view bedtime as the best time to ruminate about your day and worry about the days to come.

Unfortunately, sleep disorders have inconsistent patterns that alter your physical, mental, and emotional wellbeing. Sometimes, the problem is not even getting to sleep; it's staying asleep. While your mind is rapidly working as your body is desperately trying to find rest, it can feel like you're somewhere between sleep and hard work. You'll find yourself jumping easily at soft noises and jerking awake. Other times, this can result in you waking up grumpy and moody from lack of sufficient rest.

Sleep issues can then bring about conditions like loud snoring, sleepwalking, narcolepsy, and bruxism (grinding your teeth) (Sanghvi & Nakhat, 2020). All of these make your production level drop.

I hope at this point of the book, you are beginning to realize that unless you do something about it, your brain will simply complicate matters by continuing to produce that cortisol we talked about, making you live in constant anxiety.

3. Low self-esteem

With so many negative thoughts having a field day in your head, it's only a matter of time before you start thinking less of yourself.

To be constantly surrounded by negative premonitions is to sign up for more bad, embarrassing events that kinda justify your fear and make you a prophet of doom.

Your thoughts are untrue and unreal, but situations seem to strengthen them and make you think that all you'll ever get is disappointment and bad stuff.

Everyone makes mistakes. We all have our dirty past we run from, and we often feel disappointed longer than we should, but eventually, we must get up and move toward our goals before we get lost.

Most people will forget your shortcomings after some time since they themselves have more challenging problems to worry about. So it's a real shame that you won't let go of yours that easily and keep beating yourself up about them nonstop.

While you should think on your mistakes to avoid remaking them, when you reflect, analyze, remember, and regret them constantly, the consequences will take a toll on your self-worth because in focusing on all the wrong things you do, you won't see the other good things about yourself. It's as good as shutting the door to improvement in your own face.

4. Indecisiveness

The Stoics say when you fear the outcome of your actions without having everything you need to judge the outcome accurately, you are condemned to suffering more than you need to.

Say you want to attend a party, but you're afraid your parents might say no. Instead of simply talking to them, you begin to worry about their possible response, and your imagination runs wild: "What if my folks cut my allowance in half? What if they make me sleep in their room for the next month to ensure I don't sneak out? What if they make me get a job? What if they make me wait till 19 before I can learn to drive? What if…what if…" This continues till you get a pounding headache.

The problem is that you cannot seem to construct an appealing plea to win their approval. In your mind, whether you pitch it right or not, it won't matter. But is that really true? If they eventually say yes, you'd have suffered for nothing, and if they say no, you'd have suffered twice instead of once.

In essence, when you're indecisive because of overthinking, you're simply making yourself suffer. Make the decision anyway and then you can deal with what comes.

Your Quick Workbook: Why Won't My Mind Rest?

This first chapter's focus has been on helping you to understand the problem you're grappling with as far as overthinking is concerned.

To gain an even tighter grasp on the basics of the topic at hand, the following exercises can help you.

Let's examine how overthinking has been affecting you so far by answering the questions below.

1. When did you first notice that you have the tendency to overthink?

Answer: I first noticed this when

_____

_____

2. When you're overthinking, what common signs do you experience?

Examples of signs are:

- Throbbing headaches

- Inability to stay calm

- Horrible thoughts that won't stop

- Procrastination

- Inability to make decisions

- Sleeping issues

My symptoms:

_____

_____

3.   How do you feel after an episode of overthinking?
Common answers include:

- Stress

- Depression

- Feelings of low self-esteem

- Anger at self

- Bodily pain

Your answer:

Symptom 1: _____

Symptom 2: _____

Symptom 3: _____

Symptom 4: _____

CHAPTER TWO

"The LORD is close to the brokenhearted and saves those who are crushed in spirit."

—Psalm 34:18

CAN MY OVERTHINKING BE HELPED?

Overthinking reminds me of ants and their relentlessness. They are constantly on the move, looking for the next unfortunate insect they will overwhelm and butcher before carrying the carcass back to their colony.

It's the same thing with your thoughts. According to the Cleveland Clinic, about 60,000 thoughts are generated in your mind each day, and up to 85% of those thoughts are negative. That translates to around 48,000 negative thoughts. That's a lot of negativity, and with that in mind, it's not surprising that you overthink. Imagine one positive thought in your mind getting attacked by thousands of negative thoughts. Because of their sheer number, every ounce of positivity is overwhelmed and you're left feeling sad and disoriented.

Sound familiar?

If one didn't know better, one might think that having a life without second-guessing every decision and choice is impossible. But with the information you'll be getting in this chapter, you'll understand that for sure, it's possible to live a life without overthinking. It's fine if that sounds like a tall order to you. Just follow along with me as we unravel this mess, and by the end of this chapter, the idea won't be so farfetched to you any longer.

I FEEL LIKE I CAN'T CONTROL MY THOUGHTS!

I remember going to the birthday party of a friend's daughter. When the party was over, the girl begged her mother to allow a couple of her friends to sleep over at their house. The mother was reluctant, but the girl's pleas prevailed. Her father wasn't so thrilled about the idea either, but his wife's smooth talking on behalf of their daughter also prevailed.

If you've ever stayed back at a birthday party to clean and pack up, then you know how stressful that is. Now add to that the responsibility of watching seven additional children, all under the age of 10. Are you exhausted just thinking about it? Exactly. The kids could not be controlled. That is, until the birthday girl's father came down from his study glowering at them. One sharp command and they became quiet.

Then five minutes later they started again. The poor father came down to repeat his command, but it fell on deaf ears this time. The kids just kept on running around, shrieking and playing games. At some point, the couple and I gave up trying to control them and just took a seat and watched the kids play. There was nothing we could do to stop them, except pray for them to sleep.

Your thoughts are like those kids. Most times, there's nothing you can do to stop them from racing around in your mind, except when you sleep. Then again, sometimes sleep is not even a defense against them, as they manifest into weird dreams that have no meaning except to disturb your sleep. That just goes to show you how difficult it is to stop your thoughts.

However, not being able to stop your thoughts doesn't have to be a catastrophe. Learning how to deal with them instead just involves getting smarter since it's clear you're no match for their sheer number.

The first step in doing that is to attempt to understand the reasons why your thoughts are running wild in your mind.

Some of these reasons are explained below:

Anxiety

Anxiety is something we all experience. At its best, it helps to stir worry and alarm that there is possible danger. So you can see that it's an important emotion. At the same time, anxiety can become an unhealthy emotional reaction.

For instance, being a teenager comes with some uncertainties. Chances are that you might not feel very equipped to deal with them, and this perceived inability and lack of confidence in yourself can lead to undercurrents of anxiety or even full-blown panic attacks.

ADHD

ADHD stands for attention deficit hyperactivity disorder. It's a fairly common mental health disorder that is caused by a person's brain wiring predisposing them to being disorganized and inattentive. An important thing to note here, though, is that just because you're having a hard time concentrating in school doesn't automatically mean you are suffering from ADHD.

ADHD manifests itself in several other symptoms, including but not limited to:

1. A chronic lack of focus that results in procrastination and disorganization.

2. A lack of the kind of emotional balance appropriate for your age. ADHD slows down emotional maturity, so teens with ADHD are prone to acting out and having "temper tantrums."

3. Being highly impulsive, even more than a typical teen's level of impulsivity.

4. Being highly obsessive about one's own needs and showing no consideration for others.

Teens that suffer from ADHD have these symptoms and more occurring with more frequency and intensity in their lives, and the reason is quite simple: their thoughts are not just racing, but wandering. So it's pretty difficult to focus on one line of thought.

OCD

OCD stands for obsessive compulsive disorder. This is a mental health disorder that makes you focus on some particular thoughts or things to the point of obsession. I once met a teen who was experiencing OCD. Let's call him Shane. Shane was an athletic 16-year-old who loved basically all sports that were ever invented. And he was above average in most of them.

Here was the thing; he could never relax after a sports practice session unless his clothes were washed. And he wouldn't use the washing machine. He'd take the clothes out and wash them himself. He never trusted anyone else to do his sports laundry. All other laundry was fine, minus the sports laundry.

To everyone else, his compulsion with washing his sports clothes by himself every time might seem a tad weird. To him, it made perfect sense; he feared not performing well at games and practices, and knowing he was in ultra-clean clothes was a major performance booster for him.

OCD generally features racing thoughts on a particular topic, so you feel like you have no choice but to do whatever your obsessive thoughts compel you to do. When the action is taken, you'd feel soothed and the tension is relieved—until more obsessive thoughts arise.

PTSD

Suffering from a traumatic experience as a child can lead to post-traumatic stress disorder (PTSD). One well-known symptom of PTSD is unwelcome and intrusive thoughts. These thoughts can show up anytime, and they have an uncanny knack for being connected to the source of trauma.

For instance, a teenager whose parents got divorced when she was 9 years old is very likely to get intrusive thoughts about the situation for a long time. When she has those thoughts, they might be about her life before the divorce, how she misses spending time with her father, etc.—basically anything that will torment her and bring back some pain. This is the usual MO of intrusive thoughts as a result of PTSD, and is a major reason why sufferers of PTSD battle it for a prolonged period of time.

WHO DO I TALK TO WHO WILL UNDERSTAND?

A common problem with being a teen is not feeling like you have people to talk to. Most adults think you don't want to talk, when the actual problem is that there aren't many people who understand you enough for you to be comfortable talking to them.

As an overthinker, deciding to voice any issue at all can be fraught with a lot of mental gymnastics. It's also common to be afraid of being a bother or looking like a rambler, or worse, an idiot.

And this is exactly why many teens who overthink struggle to speak with anyone about their overthinking. But this is what you have to know: no one can function **effectively** as a loner. Nature proves it; animals that hunt in packs have a statistically better chance of finding some food than solitary hunters.

It doesn't matter if people don't understand you. Heck, they don't even understand themselves some of the time. Just focus on finding the one person who does understand you and love you enough to listen. Sometimes such people might be your parents or siblings or another family member. Sometimes it might be your best friend.

And sometimes, it might be a therapist. Now, I know speaking to a therapist most likely isn't on your bucket list, but they're not half bad. They're trained to listen and provide guidance to help you find answers to your burning questions.

Also, a key benefit of talking to someone about your overthinking is that a fresh set of eyes can help you see a perspective you didn't know was possible.

I also know someone else you can speak to who will definitely understand: yourself. No one else understands you better than you. You can get a diary and transfer your thoughts from your head to your book, asking and analyzing until it makes sense.

Writing down your thoughts may help you organize them. It also helps you single out the tormenting thoughts. For instance, making a mistake usually results in a lot of thoughts that are very harmful and judgmental.

When you're writing down such thoughts, think of one incident of weakness that you think makes you a terrible person. Write it down and try to answer questions like: If I was a different person, would I have acted the same way? If I knew the whole story, would I have acted differently? Would I have acted differently if this had happened on a different day, at a different time, with a different group of people?

If you cannot answer "yes" to all those questions, then you have no right to judge your character or identity based on that mistake.

The point here is that talking to yourself can go a long, long way. It can help you see things clearer and can be surprisingly good for venting.

CAN OVERTHINKING BE CURED? (A LOOK AT THE ROLE OF ENDORPHINS AND OTHER CHEMICALS)

You already know what cortisol can do in the brain, but the essence of this book is to give you solutions, so you also want to know about the other chemicals in the body that can alleviate or aggravate the overthinking problem.

The hormones in our body send signals to the different parts, regulating growth, metabolic processes, and moods.

An imbalanced hormone level can interrupt the average growth and metabolic process, and it can also cause complications with our moods. Your overthinking and anxiety could be hormonal sometimes, so it is essential to walk you through how hormones in the body can affect our thoughts.

The sex hormones are testosterone and estrogen, and they affect how we overthink and get anxious when changes occur during puberty and, for females, during menstruation.

Estrogen is the female sex hormone that secretes more serotonin chemicals during the first two weeks of the (on average) 28-day menstrual cycle than in the last weeks if the woman does not get pregnant. It is the underlying reason girls have mood swings during their period because levels of serotonin, one of the happiness hormones, drop when the egg is not fertilized and the lining of the uterus is subsequently shed during menstruation.

In males, on the other hand, a reduction in testosterone production can lead to depression, anxiety, mood swings, and irritability, making you more likely to overly consider tiny details that don't matter.

Cortisol is a stress hormone, and as has already been mentioned, it is released to warn against impending danger. Adrenaline is similar to cortisol, initiating the "flight or fight" response to help the body manage threats and prepare for war if necessary.

Oxytocin is a love hormone released when we are having a good time or feeling loved. It calms the body and reduces anxiety when secreted. The level of oxytocin in the body increases when we hug someone we feel safe with or kiss our spouse, for example. When we cuddle up with a person we care about, we release oxytocin, which can lead to a drop in anxiety, aggression, and feelings of depression.

This does not stop with behavior alone. If we engage good thoughts also, we promote the secretion of oxytocin and improve the chances of eradicating those negative thoughts that cripple our minds.

The most important thing to note is that most times, we are at the mercy of our hormones. Those imbalances will occur with little or no interference from us, and when they do, they slice through our joy and poke holes in our serenity, leaving us anxious and moody. But now, we know that there are other hormones that, if we do certain things or force ourselves to think specific thoughts, can help us mitigate the effects of anxiety, overthinking, and depression.

You should also note that this knowledge suggests intentionality. This is just one thing you can do amongst several others, but at this point, you need to recognize that you have a role in consciously and deliberately helping yourself in situations of overthinking.

What To Avoid

As we close in on what you can do for yourself, you must know what to avoid and never engage in under the guise of seeking solutions to your issue.

The first thing you want to avoid is drugs, primarily because you are too young for those shenanigans, and secondly, because they are no good in the long run.

Even though your heart may be racing and feels like it will jump out of your chest, or even if you have stayed up most nights for two weeks due to anxiety, even if your eyelids are swollen from crying at night before you go to sleep and after you wake up, avoid drugs. They are too addictive and it is simply too risky to get involved; you're more likely to pick up more problems through drug use than you had before you started.

I say this not because I don't understand your exhaustion and helplessness. On the contrary, I say this because I *do* understand.

Alcohol is not a good idea either. It is a depressant that tampers with the speed of your brain and nervous system processes. It makes you feel bold and suppresses your anxiety and fears, only to release them once the alcohol wears off. When they come rushing back, you'll be triggered to go back to the alcohol to suppress those feelings, and the cycle continues.

Do not practice escapism. Just like drug and alcohol abuse, it is an attempt to suppress what is real. Escapism builds up fantasies that restrict your fears and worries while permitting thoughts that bring a feeling of satisfaction. It causes you to evade real problems that need attending to.

Sure, sometimes escaping our thoughts can be a good thing. It can allow our bodies to rejuvenate from stress and return to the inevitable fight of life stronger, healthier, and better. It allows us to deal with overwhelming thoughts and clear brain blocks that prevent our creativity from working productively. But it becomes unhealthy when we begin to procrastinate, deny reality, and disobey social rules and norms that preserve life. When it becomes your first answer to real problems, it becomes unhealthy.

If you desire to come out of this tunnel of darkness into light, you must not engage in any of these, because ignoring the truth does not make a lie the truth. In the same way, suppressants will not get you to safety, so you must be willing to take the long walk to freedom—long but worth every bit of time and energy.

Overthinking Can Be Cured

Studies have shown that overthinking is prevalent in young adults ages 25-35 and older adults ages 45-55, which makes the delicate age bracket of teens more complicated to deal with. But no matter the stats, overthinking clearly is better tackled when it's still in its infancy, and that's mostly when it shows up in your life as a teenager.

Contrary to what many people think, teens are highly pleasant humans that are also greatly malleable. There's the indisputable stubbornness and bullheadedness which many adults find insulting, but behind that steely exterior is a mushy, kind, and eager-to-learn teenager. That teenager is malleable and willing to be taught.

As long as that part of you exists, you can get over your overthinking issues in no time. And that's the catch: staying interested in learning.

Maneuvering your mind as a teen is easier because you have formed fewer brain patterns that automate your daily routines, so there is more room for new habits and value formation to help you snap out of overthinking.

There is hope for you, and I say this with total sincerity. I am cheering for you, and I firmly believe that you will make the right choices about finding healing.

Your Quick Workbook: I Just Need Someone to Understand Me

1. Is there someone in your life whom you've talked to in the past about your problems as a teenager— someone who totally gets your struggles?

Your answer:

_____

_____

_____ (Note: It can be a parent, guardian, family member, friend, teacher, therapist, or even yourself)

2. Earlier in the chapter, we talked about writing to yourself in a journal. Have you ever tried journaling? If so, how did it feel?

Your answer:

_____

_____

3. Who do you think you can talk to about your overthinking issues now that will understand? Put down their name and why you think they're a great pick. For example, if you write "Aunt Lucy will be a great person to talk to about this," also include the reason (e.g., "She doesn't judge me. She's an experienced therapist and I can trust her to keep this between us.")

Your answer:

_____

_____

4. What do you hope to say to this person when you meet with them?

Your answer:

_____

_____

5. Do you believe that therapy is going to help you beat overthinking?

Your answer:

_____

_____

CHAPTER THREE

"Be strong and courageous, do not be afraid or tremble at them, for the LORD your God is the one who goes with you. He will not fail you or forsake you."

—Deuteronomy 31:6

CHECKING FOR UNDERLYING PROBLEMS AND MENTAL HEALTH ISSUES

Phew! So far so good. We seem to be making some progress, don't we? In this chapter, we'll take a look at the problems and mental issues that can either cause overthinking or make it worse. You might already be familiar with some of them, but even if you aren't, trust that I'm going to be making them as easy as possible for you to grasp.

Perfectionism and an over-achieving nature

Perfectionism is often intertwined with an over-achieving nature. The desire to achieve against all odds can make you insist on perfection or nothing else—which isn't always a bad thing, but this behavior often comes with high-functioning anxiety.

A perfectionist might try to hide their anxiety, but when they're stricken with worry, fear, and their vision of perfection, the frustration they experience from trying to do everything perfectly and achieve better results than everyone else leads to overthinking, and ultimately ends up crippling them.

While their results are sometimes extraordinary, perfectionists don't see what's so bad about their approach because they perceive their method of striving for perfection as necessary to reach the top. However, perfectionist behavior can make overthinking worse. The constant, insatiable reach for "perfection" and flawlessness can eventually steal peace and tranquility from anyone's mind.

PTSD

As we've discussed earlier in this book, post-traumatic stress disorder is an anxiety disorder that follows a traumatic event or abuse. People who have experienced trauma are highly susceptible to overthinking through no fault of their own. Whatever kind of abuse or trauma you've suffered, it can cause you a lot of fear and negative thoughts, which may culminate into post-traumatic stress disorder. From experiencing natural disasters to being involved in a horrific car accident to being the victim of an abusive relationship, PTSD can arise from a wide range of traumatic experiences.

A study published in the psychiatry journal *Child and Adolescent Mental Health* found that PTSD begins for children when they cannot process their trauma. If they aren't given help to figure things out, they begin to interpret their trauma symptoms as a personal failure, and it negatively impacts their self-worth (Dyregrov & Yule, 2006). The tendency to interpret PTSD as a weakness or something shameful is in itself a problem because that only strengthens the symptoms and prolongs the recovery process.

Depending on the level of fear and pain experienced during trauma or abuse, the symptoms of post-traumatic stress disorder do not generally linger long after the trauma if they are appropriately addressed, treated, and managed. But if not addressed, they can quickly become a big problem and provide fertile ground for overthinking.

If you had issues with overthinking before experiencing a trauma, that overthinking will likely be worsened by the PTSD.

The classic signs that you're dealing with PTSD as a teenager include constant flashbacks and nightmares that give you scary replays of the trauma or abuse you experienced. Hypervigilance (that is, being constantly alert and sensitive to potential danger or harm around you) is another sign. Then there's the tendency to have a predominantly negative outlook on life. However intense your PTSD symptoms might be, whether mild or severe, PTSD could be an underlying reason for the constant overthinking you're going through.

Obsessive-compulsive disorder

Before we jump into a description of this disorder, let's take a look at how it manifests in real life.

Esther's Story

Every night before I go to sleep, I check that the gas is off. I also make sure that the doors are locked and that the water heater is ready to kick on in the morning. I check the oven and look out the window to confirm that I rolled up the car windows in case it rains overnight and, of course, to prevent my car from being stolen. But this is just the first round of checking.

Two hours after I get into bed to sleep, I'm still wide awake, wondering if I actually did roll up the car windows. The fear that I've forgotten to do so grips me. I imagine that my car has probably already been stolen and that the thief has set fire to my apartment, which will surely blow up in a bit because I left the gas on. I bolt out of bed and race to the kitchen to find the gas safely turned off, my car sitting in the garage with the windows rolled up, and everything else exactly the way I left it.

But the moment I return to my room, the cycle starts all over again, and I can't help but imagine the worst case scenario. Most nights, I jump out of bed to check at least three times because I can't remember whether I turned off something or another. It's terribly exhausting, and I'm at my wit's end with it.

This is obsessive-compulsive disorder (OCD) at work, causing unwanted, persistent nagging thoughts and desires that affect a person's daily routine. When I spoke with Esther, she was 23 at the time and living alone, but she'd been having this problem since she was 14 years old.

People with obsessive-compulsive disorder may constantly check their belongings to see if anything has gone missing or been tampered with. OCD is a stressful condition that can intensify overthinking, as OCD-driven thoughts are usually horrific and intrusive, driving the person with this condition to repeat certain compulsive behaviors to relieve their anxiety.

People suffering with OCD may also hoard worn-out and useless items because of their desire to keep everything they have safe. Losing things can cause anxiety and distress. In the end, the thinking patterns of people with OCD are similar to those of someone with a tendency to overthink. Overthinking and OCD combined create what I regard as the biggest mental mess ever.

Depression

It is difficult to tell whether overthinking comes before depression or depression before overthinking, but they are closely related.

Experiencing sadness is part of living and growing up, so it is not unusual. What is unusual is getting stuck in a bad mood until your mood falls entirely and constantly below normal. Symptoms like losing enthusiasm about life altogether, chronic sadness, bitterness, irritation, lack of desire to get out of bed, worry, no longer enjoying what used to make you happy, and an inability to think indicate depression. When you dwell on a bad feeling for several days, it's a sign that you are overthinking and heading towards depression.

When your mood falls to the point where even positive events do not affect it, to the point of losing interest in fun things or feeling anger, hopelessness, and fatigue all the time, then there's a problem. Depression can certainly make your overthinking issues even worse.

Anxiety

As we have discussed, anxiety is a feeling of constant fear and worry. It is a response to fear, which is supposed to be a good thing because fear warns you that there is an incoming danger and you need to either escape or resist.

But fear and worry (anxiety) about every little thing might lead to overthinking. You do not have to worry about making a decision or trying something new. Anxiety over everyday decisions may arise from time to time, but if the worry lingers and becomes paralyzing, it can create a negative spiral of overthinking.

Identity crisis

If you lose your sense of who you are, you will be in for an uncomfortable ride. Having a stable identity means having a healthy perception of your past and present selves and an objective for your future self.

Having a stable identity also involves not changing your mind about who you are, your values, or your morals just because of what someone said or did to you. If a person makes a negative statement about your identity, being able to stand your ground without second-guessing yourself is a sign that you are confident and comfortable in your identity.

If you scream at your dad, yell at your younger sister, and give your mom the silent treatment for days until she gives in to what you want, but meanwhile you go to school, have fun with your friends, and act nice to your crush— you should take time to think about your identity.

An identity crisis is a state of confusion about several aspects of your life. For a teen like you, the different ways you feel at home and in school can begin to disturb your opinion of your identity, especially if your childhood environment did not foster stable self-awareness.

Each stage of our psychosocial development builds on the previous one, and a problem in one stage can disturb the balance and alter our sense of satisfaction with our identity. In the teenage years, however, we reach the level of "identity against role confusion"; in this stage, it is important that you stay loyal to yourself (Dyregrov & Yule, 2006). Some overthinking during your teenage years is normal as you discover who you are, but if you experience a great deal of confusion about your identity during this time, it may lead to excessive overthinking.

Stress

The feeling of stress is similar to anxiety—physical and emotional tiredness. Like anxiety, it is your body's way of warning you to avoid danger.

Stress can be acute or chronic. It is acute when it goes away quickly, whereas chronic stress stays with you for much longer. Acute stress is the stress you experience when you fight with your siblings or speed up your pace to catch up with someone, or the feeling you get when your teacher announces a pop quiz in class.

Chronic stress, however, occurs when you are bothered about something for days or even months on end. If your teacher picks on you in class, that can stress you chronically. If your parents are going through a divorce, that can cause you chronic stress too. This kind of lingering chronic stress can make overcoming overthinking more complicated for you.

Low self-esteem

A lowered self-worth can be another reason that you might be overthinking simple suggestions to go out and have fun or live a little.

Overthinking can lower your self-esteem, but low self-esteem also creates more overthinking. It deprives you of participating in challenging tasks because you just don't believe you have what it takes to be successful. The negative thoughts we harbor make our self-worth drop; worrying too much about your appearance, past behavior, or mistakes only keeps you down unnecessarily.

A large percentage of what you need to build confidence and self-worth comes from the things you hear most often from your parents, teachers, siblings, and friends. Thus, if your parents, peers, or authority figures in your life are constantly tearing you down, you might have a harder time building up your self-esteem.

Low self-esteem can cause a repeated pattern of failure and disappointment; consequently, you'll overthink those terrible experiences and the cycle will continue.

Takeaway

There are several mental health issues that could be fueling your overthinking problem, and this should tell you that if you want to live a good life free of overthinking, you'll need to put in a lot of work and energy. You need to confront these mental battles at an early age to help you overcome them more easily.

Your Quick Workbook: Dealing with Underlying Issues

1. What underlying issues have you noticed that could be making your overthinking worse?

Underlying issues:

1. _____

2. _____

3. _____

2. Examine your stress levels: Do you often overthink because you're stressed about something, especially things people have said about you? Write down some examples.

Your answer:

_____

_____

3. Would you say that you're battling with depression alongside overthinking? What are the signs?

Your answer:

_____

_____

Part 2

Yes, There Are Solutions!

Aproblem shared is half-solved. True. But half-solving this problem of overthinking is not what we're gunning for.

As wonderful as it is to dissect a problem and understand it, that's not enough. Going from there, solutions should be sought. That's what we're about to do, so we're in business.

The solutions to overthinking lie in making a few things work. From challenging cognitive distortions to building your self-confidence, a few things will need to shift. These comprehensive solutions require your willingness and cooperation. But trust me, it'll all be worth it.

CHAPTER FOUR

"For you, O Lord, are my hope, my trust, O Lord, from my youth."

—Psalm 71:5

DEVELOPING YOUR SELF-CONFIDENCE: A FULL GUIDE

Louie's Story

Self-confidence?

No kidding; the first time I heard this word, I literally went, "Seriously?" I mean, SELF-confidence? Like, confidence in yourself? People did that?

You might be surprised at why I was so shocked about something so simple. Upon first considering it, self-confidence doesn't sound like rocket science or anything. Until you have to put it into practice. For me, the entire idea of having any sort of belief in my abilities was torn to shreds at the beginning of middle school. Years later, I still remember the defining incident clearly, as though it happened just yesterday.

The reading comprehension teacher had given us a passage to read and answer a few questions. I wasn't really interested in reading comprehension, but I had to do the assignment anyway. After I got home the day the assignment was given, I received the shock of my life: my parents were getting divorced. My mom tried to reassure me that I'd still be able to see my dad and get to hang out with him, but I was inconsolable. I had classmates whose parents were divorced, and I knew how unhappy it made them.

It was in this kind of atmosphere that I had to do my assignments, including the reading comprehension one. The next week in class, the teacher called me up to read my answers. Reluctantly, I walked to the front and stammered badly, eventually bursting into tears after a few attempts. I was thoroughly embarrassed, and even a couple of my friends made fun of me. But all I could think of was my parents and their betrayal and that we were no longer a family.

Despite my pleas, they stayed divorced, and I eventually got over the pain. But I never got over the embarrassment of standing in front of the class and making a fool of myself.

The "self" topics have become really popular these days. Self-love, self-esteem, self-worth, self-compassion…the list is endless. When you look at it, a critical question that comes to mind is: Are we getting more selfish as we keep bringing up so much talk about "self"? Or have we been too selfless and we're finally realizing the importance of looking inwards, hence the popular revolution of "self" topics?

Well, I don't know what the answer to that is. Maybe you can get in touch with me if you do. But I know that these "self" topics have never been more important. The current world is so fast-paced that we often forget to take care of ourselves. We forget to love ourselves, nurture ourselves, and even praise ourselves for little jobs well done. If you're having issues with overthinking as a teenager, chances are that you've joined our fast-paced world and are neglecting some very crucial parts of your own growth and development. Chances are that it's not just that your mind is constantly racing but that you're constantly seeing yourself in a not-so-good light. Chances are that you don't trust your own judgment. Can't blame you for getting caught up in this mess. You're here looking for a solution, and that's enough.

Self-confidence is a tricky thing. For something so crucial to success in life, it's easily affected by many different factors. Mostly, it's about the quality of your thoughts about yourself. It's really as straightforward as it sounds—having confidence in yourself—but "self" is a very powerful word that comprises complex concepts.

Like a domino chain where one thing leads to another, self-confidence cannot exist in isolation. It's deeply intertwined with the other parts of your mind, experiences, beliefs, habits, and cognition. No matter how determined you are to build your self-confidence, you won't get there until you accept these basic facts.

As a teenager, you're facing and will face a variety of issues that will test your confidence. How you deal with those issues will be a testament to your readiness to hone this skill. One example of this is people's perception of your appearance and how you handle both solicited and unsolicited comments from people about your looks.

Self-confidence can easily originate from perception. If you perceive that others think you look good, your self-confidence will likely be high. But if you perceive that you don't fit into the societal (and often unrealistic) standards for looks, then chances are that your self-confidence will be low. That's why you might feel more comfortable and happier when socializing if you're wearing something expensive; you perceive that people want to talk to you and wish to identify with you because of how you look, and that boosts your confidence. At the same time, if you've been body-shamed in the past, or don't have many nice clothes to wear, your self-confidence might be impacted. To make things even more complex, I've seen people without nice clothes who can stand in front of any audience and give a confident speech, and I've also seen rich or "popular" kids who can't hold their own in a small roundtable conversation. So when I say it's a perception thing, it's actually about *your* perception, not the perception of others.

With low self-confidence comes an increase in overthinking, as you'll spend more time wondering about how people view you, what they think about you, how your choices will impact their view of you, and so on. Your thoughts will go blah, blah, blah, up and down, back and forth…hardly looking at facts but fixated on false ideas and worries about what others think.

If you want to achieve self-confidence and feel good in your own skin, it has to begin with you. It's you who must be ready to think well of yourself first, before expecting anyone else to do so. You must nurture a better and more positive view of yourself, and your strengths and weaknesses alike. When you feel more comfortable in yourself, you'll find it easier to kick overthinking out of the way and begin to live your life to the fullest. We'll be dealing with all that this entails in the next couple of pages.

What is self-confidence?

Self-confidence is your attitude towards your own skills and abilities; it is the degree to which you accept and trust yourself based on how you perceive your own abilities (University of South Florida, n.d.). If you perceive yourself favorably, you'll trust your sense of judgment and feel more in control of your life. But if your perception of yourself and your abilities is not favorable, then you'll definitely battle with low self-confidence.

Being able to communicate confidently and handle criticism is also a gauge of your self-confidence. With low self-confidence, a constant feeling of self-doubt is not far behind, alongside a likely difficulty in trusting others. You're also likely to feel inferior and unloved.

What are the causes of low self-confidence? There are many things that can lead to low self-confidence, but I've listed a few of them below:

- Judging yourself too harshly for mistakes

Over and over again, you might have heard of the importance of cutting yourself some slack. Except that you don't do it. But the truth is that it's the best way to live. No matter how efficient or competent you are, you're bound to make mistakes. As a teenager with so many life choices ahead of you, making decisions will naturally come with a few blunders along the way.

You're young. You've got this. You can't allow yourself to get overly critical of everything you do, even if you make an actual mistake. Self-criticism is like a cancer that eats up self-confidence, and if you're dealing with little to no confidence, you should check how much criticism you're serving yourself in a day. You've probably had enough by now.

- Growing up in a toxic environment

The number of people in the world who come from fully functional families where abuse and toxicity was not present is very small. Go check out how many people are reading *Adult Children of Emotionally Immature Parents* and you'll see what I mean. Many teens and young adults have already been through so much trauma that all they can manage now is therapy.

If you're among this class of people, you'll relate to the idea that self-confidence feels like a luxury because the environment that you grew up in didn't foster it.

- Being afraid of failure and judgment

A lack of self-confidence indicates an absence of self-praise. If you don't believe in yourself, then you won't take risks. The fear of failure and judgment from others can cause a significant drop in your confidence.

Moving along now. There are three things that are important for you to note about self-confidence:

1. Self-confidence is based on your perception of your abilities

2. Self-confidence can be situational or total

3. Self-confidence is based on your trust in your abilities

Let me get into explaining what I mean.

1. Self-confidence is based on your perception of your abilities

In a way, self-confidence is not a real thing. It's all based on perception, which can be true or exaggerated positively or negatively. Your level of self-perception is largely a result of three factors:

- how you think you appear to others
- how you think others appraise your appearance and abilities
- pride or shame based on your perception of the appraisal of other people

For many people, their level of self-perception is very low, and so they tend to shrink from any situation that will put pressure on them to use their abilities. This is, in a way, logical thinking, because if you don't believe you're capable of anything useful, then chances are you won't want to do anything remotely useful with yourself.

This is why many people with low self-confidence tend to exhibit one or more of the following characteristics:

- Social withdrawal and anxiety
- Lack of social skills

- Depression

- Inability to accept compliments

- Inability to be fair to yourself

- Self-neglect

On the other hand, having high self-perception is key to nurturing a healthy level of self-confidence. If you think other people perceive you highly, you're likely to feel pride from the appraisal of other people, and this will feed your level of self-confidence.

2. Self-confidence can be situational or total

Again, this fact about self-confidence is linked to how you feel about your abilities. We all have strengths and weaknesses in different areas of life, and if you're put in a situation where you have to function with your weaknesses, chances are that you'll feel very self-conscious and low on confidence.

This is an example of situational low self-confidence. It's different from feeling low self-confidence all the time, almost like it's on default mode in your brain.

3. Self-confidence is based on your trust in your abilities

Everyone knows a Ferrari is faster than a Camry. If both cars were to be in a race, I'd be willing to bet $500,000 that the driver of the Ferrari would feel pretty confident about his/her chances of winning the race. (Never mind whether or not I actually have that much money to place on a bet.)

This is the same thing with self-confidence. With a high level of trust in your abilities comes an inherent ease in doing what you're supposed to do.

Again, this just goes to show that your perception of yourself and how others see you, alongside the resulting trust or lack thereof in your abilities, is really the major make-up of your level of self-confidence.

Relating self-confidence issues to overthinking

The problem with overthinking, again, is not just that you spend a lot of time thinking about the past; it is that you also do the same thing about the present and the future. For instance, imagine thinking about an event that is going to take place a few days from now and the various parts of that event that you cannot control. As a result of thinking about these things, you'll be very nervous about the actual event and might even dread the event happening. All these feelings are bound to knock your level of self-confidence down a few notches.

This results in feeling insecure about yourself, inept, or clumsy. These feelings don't reflect the true you, but they will become your perception of yourself and will determine how you'll act. Convincing yourself that you're not worth anything, even though that is clearly a lie, is usually a result of overthinking.

There are three common mistakes you may make when judging yourself as an overthinker, and these mistakes cause a massive drop in your self-confidence. They are:

Mistake 1: Judging yourself incorrectly

A couple of weeks ago, a teen asked me this question: Why do we judge ourselves harshly for past mistakes when we know it will affect our self-confidence?

It was a bit of a headscratcher at first, but here's my answer: we don't like to admit that we all make mistakes. Admitting that you might be wrong, even to yourself, takes a lot of self-acceptance, which is not something a lot of people have developed. Making mistakes is a human thing; we cannot always tell what the right response is for every situation. Of course, with making mistakes comes the inevitable feeling of being unhappy with yourself for the mistake, negative self-talk that tears you down, etc. But in spite of these negative side effects of making mistakes, doing so can be quite good for your learning, and that is the approach you should take to making mistakes.

Be determined to learn from your mistakes and let go of them. In truth, most of our mistakes are not even remembered by the people we made the mistakes around, so focusing on them for a long period of time is not really helpful for you. You'd only be dwelling on a single moment in your life and magnifying it unnecessarily.

For instance, imagine you accidentally bump into someone at a restaurant and make them spill their coffee. You apologize and the person says it's okay. It should ordinarily end there, right? Wrong. For an overthinker, you'll probably go home and wonder all day (and probably all night) about whether the person thinks you're a clumsy fool. Thousands of racing thoughts would flow in the direction of this biased thinking pattern and reinforce the erroneous idea that you're clumsy. From there, your self-confidence begins to get chipped away—all because of a mistake that the person who was affected probably doesn't even remember any longer.

This is why the best thing to do with any mistake you make is to learn from it. Learning from your mistakes helps you become more observant about yourself and your behaviors, so you can reduce the chances of making the same mistake in future. It also frankly helps you get much-needed peace of mind if you make a mistake, as you're more likely to focus on what you can change rather than past events you have no control over.

Mistake 2: Focusing on things you can't control

In spite of all of humanity's advancement, there are so many things that are completely out of our control, both as a race and as individuals. For instance, no one on this ball of rock can control what family or circumstances he/she is born into.

Something I have noticed is that to compensate for the knowledge that we actually have shockingly little control over our own lives, we worry. And as an overthinker, you're more likely to be better acquainted with worry than the average person. For instance, imagine you have a school presentation coming up. You're well prepared when it comes to the material for the presentation, but you're all over the place mentally, running though all sorts of improbable scenarios in which the presentation could go wrong. You're worried sick about things that might not even be realistic, and as a result you create this sort of self-fulfilling prophecy where you go into the presentation thinking you're unqualified to handle it or something equally untrue.

The result of this kind of mental torture is often that you give up before you've even started, and this would most likely lead to a terrible presentation—not because you were not capable, but because of unnecessary worry.

So you can see that worrying about what you cannot control is not only pointless, but also harmful. Worrying incessantly about things that are out of your control will also result in going through life as an anxious person. You'll never be able to truly relax and settle, never be able to grow and enjoy life.

Instead of worrying, it's often much better to plan. There's a thin line between worrying and planning, and the difference is the acceptance of the fact that you cannot plan for everything. So you plan for what you can control, and you let the rest go.

When you plan properly, you feel better prepared and less anxious. A lower degree of anxiety means a higher degree of self-confidence, which is the whole point.

Mistake 3: Holding on to grudges

Forgiveness is a big part of human interaction. Without it, human civilization as we know it would have fallen apart a long time ago. Why? Let's face it; sometimes, humans can be jerks, including us. And so we need the offended person to forgive us so the crack in the relationship is restored and all is back to what it was.

In situations where forgiveness is withheld, it can easily lead to a breakdown of the relationship, no matter how important the relationship is. Of course, it is very important to keep evaluating your relationships and break off toxic ones, but it is often best to do everything you can to mend the relationship when offenses happen. If you're the one who is wrong, it actually takes a healthy level of self-confidence to admit this and seek forgiveness. The same thing goes for if you're the one who was wronged. Blindly seeking revenge or holding resentment against the other party will just amount to a lot of bitterness and anxiety, eventually causing a drain on your self-confidence. I'll explain how.

Have you ever been so angry at someone that you don't even want to see the person? Exactly. This kind of situation causes a lot of anxiety because behind the anger is a lot of hurt and shame, and the mere thought of seeing the person brings you face to face with a situation you would prefer not to face. The funny thing is many of the people we typically dislike in life are people that, for one reason or another, we can't avoid, such as a neighbor, a relative, or a classmate.

What happens when you have to face them? Your anxiety level spikes because instinctively you know the situation is not one you can control, and your self-confidence drops as a result. If you are forced to keep meeting this person who is a stressor to you, chances are that eventually you'll do something rash out of bitterness and resentment, and then sabotage any possibility of ever recovering the relationship.

But what if instead of all this ruckus and damage to your self-confidence, you chose to ignore the person and just focus on your own happiness? Focusing too much on the offense done to you will lead you to hold a grudge against the person, overthink the person's bad behavior and give yourself a lot of headaches. I believe it's much better for you to choose yourself and your happiness, and focus more on that. If this means forgiving others, then do it. You'll be better off for it. "Let all bitterness, wrath, anger, clamor, and evil speaking be put away from you, with all malice. And be kind to one another, tenderhearted, forgiving one another, even as God in Christ forgave you"—Ephesians 4:31, 32.

HOW TO DEVELOP SELF-CONFIDENCE USING A STEP-BY-STEP CBT APPROACH

The importance of having a good dose of self-confidence cannot be overemphasized. But what if your self-confidence is currently on the floor, and you need to get it back up?

I've got just the thing for you. Say hello to cognitive behavioral therapy, or CBT for short.

CBT is a psychological treatment method that helps to improve mental health issues, including depression, eating disorders, and anxiety disorders, to mention a few.

This method works based on the idea that your feelings, thoughts, and behaviors are all linked. So if you think in a particular direction, you're very likely to have feelings that support that thinking pattern, and your behavior will subsequently reflect it. Therefore, CBT helps you identify and replace the negative thoughts that are generated automatically in your mind with helpful ones.

CBT is typically very structured and the sessions are generally short, but it does pack a serious punch in terms of eliminating negative thinking patterns. As a teen and an overthinker, you probably find it very easy to slip into negative thinking patterns that cause distortions in the way you perceive yourself. Using CBT techniques, a psychotherapist will help you pinpoint the negative thoughts that cause overthinking and negative thinking patterns.

The following are just a few of the benefits of using CBT:

- Better communication skills
- Identification of negative thoughts and replacement with positive ones
- Improvement in mood

- Improvement in self-confidence

CBT is one of the most popular methods for therapy, and that's why I personally recommend it for teens who need help with depression, self-esteem issues, self-confidence, anxiety disorders, etc.

Practicing the principles of CBT to build your self-confidence can be done by following these simple and highly effective steps. I recommend you take each point as a mini session, and have a pen and paper handy each time you're going through a session. If one session is not enough to treat a point, then schedule another.

In this way, you'll be able to maximize this step-by-step framework.

1. Identify negative thinking patterns

The foundation of everything wrong with your self-confidence is your negative thinking patterns; the chain of those thought patterns has to be broken. Breaking the chain requires a lot of self-awareness, as you have to consciously observe the negative patterns and note them down. Obviously, observing your thoughts as an overthinker can be a pretty tricky thing to do, but it's not impossible.

The key is not to actually observe each thought, but to observe the mental messages you are transmitting. For instance, if you think you're a failure, then you're going to have a lot of thoughts dedicated to reinforcing that negative message. This is a negative thinking pattern. Once you can pinpoint the message you're transmitting, then step one is done.

It is often a good idea to write down the message so you can try to pinpoint where it originated from. For instance, if you always feel like you're a failure after algebra class, then it's safe to say algebra class is a stressor for you.

2. Find the purpose of the thinking pattern

There's this phrase I love a lot: if purpose is not known, abuse is inevitable. Thinking should always be done with a purpose, and if you apply this mindset to negative thinking patterns, then their hold on you starts to unravel.

You can ask yourself the following questions to determine the purpose of any negative thinking pattern:

- Is this thinking pattern trying to protect me in any way?

- ○ If yes, how is it protecting me?

- ○ If no, then what is the usefulness of this thinking pattern?

- ▪ Is the protection from this thinking pattern hindering me in any way?

For instance, suppose the thinking pattern you have identified is one that says you're a failure. Now, that is obviously a negative thinking pattern, but it is still wise to find out the purpose.

So, applying the questions above to that thinking pattern, below are likely answers:

- ▪ Is this thinking pattern trying to protect me in any way? **No.**

- ▪ Then what is the usefulness of this thinking pattern? **It has no usefulness to me.**

This is a systematic and problem-based approach to dislodging unhealthy and unhelpful thinking patterns.

3. Consider evidence against the negative thinking pattern

This step is to help you strengthen your grip on dislodging negative thinking patterns. Getting evidence against your negative thinking patterns will help you get a firm grip on why those patterns have to be changed.

Going with our earlier example, imagine you already know that thinking you're a failure doesn't help you, nor does it protect you. The next thing to do is to challenge the claim and write down things you do well. Doesn't matter what it is; as long as you do it well, then write it down.

Say you have five things you do very well. Those are five proofs that you are not a failure. Take a little while to revel in the knowledge that you actually have things you do well.

4. Challenge your inner critic

Everyone has a small part of themselves that offers constant criticism. To this inner critic, it's basically like you can't do anything well, no matter how hard you try. Your mistakes are overemphasized and your achievements are underemphasized. You actually can't win with this voice. The good news is that your inner critic is highly illogical, so logic is a very good weapon to weaken its hold on you.

Doing this entails challenging your inner critic. Your inner critic is the primary source of negative and unhealthy thoughts, so challenging it can be a bit overwhelming at first. It is very important to take this step by step, so as not to defeat the purpose of the whole process.

The way to do this is simple; separate your thoughts from the constantly negative chatter of your inner critic.

The following questions will help you achieve this effectively:

- Is this negative self-talk from my inner critic objective and true?

- Is there any objective evidence to <u>support</u> this negative self-talk from my inner critic?

- Is there any objective evidence to <u>dispute</u> this negative self-talk from my inner critic?

- What does the actual evidence say about this thought?

Example 1

Let's take our earlier example of you thinking you're a failure and how this thought pattern is reinforced by your inner critic.

Negative thought pattern: I am a failure

Situation: I flunked my algebra test.

Is this negative self-talk from my inner critic objective and true: No. It's true that I flunked algebra, but I didn't flunk other subjects. I haven't failed in all areas of my life.

Is there any objective evidence to <u>support</u> this negative self-talk from my inner critic: I did not pass my algebra test.

Is there any objective evidence to <u>dispute</u> this negative self-talk from my inner critic: I passed all my other tests. I had As in the majority of my tests.

What does the actual evidence say about this thought: Actual evidence says this thought makes no sense because I passed other subjects. If I were to be a failure truly, I'd fail in all other areas.

Example 2

Negative thought pattern: Nothing in my life goes right. Everything is falling apart. I hate my life.

Situation: My parents are getting divorced.

Is this negative self-talk from my inner critic objective and true: No. My parents' divorce may be difficult, even painful to deal with, but it wasn't my fault. Their love life isn't something I can control. My parents are an important part of my life, but I have to live my own life. My life is not falling apart.

Is there any objective evidence to <u>support</u> this negative self-talk from my inner critic: My parents are getting a divorce.

Is there any objective evidence to <u>dispute</u> this negative self-talk from my inner critic: They're my parents. My life is not bound to fall apart because of their relationship's failure.

What does the actual evidence say about this thought: Accepting my parents' divorce may be hard, but my whole life isn't just comprised of my parents. I have school, my friends, my own relationships, and other things going on as well.

5. Consider a healthier thought you can believe

The point of CBT is not just for you to identify distorted thinking patterns. For the process to be complete and for your self-confidence level to rise, it is important that you replace the negative thought pattern with a positive and healthy one.

Going by our first example, let's say you have been able to successfully challenge your inner critic, and you recognize that the truth of the matter is that you are not a failure just because you flunked algebra.

A healthy thought pattern would be to start thinking this way and appreciate the fact that you passed other subjects. To further strengthen this idea, you can promise yourself to do better on your next algebra test. This way, your thinking pattern is geared towards positivity.

Wrapping up

It is important to note that a low level of self-confidence cannot be increased overnight. Years of negative thinking and critical self-talk will have to be worked on consciously and systematically for a while till you start seeing changes.

Keep at it and you'll start to see improvements day after day. That little forward motion you're making, no matter how small it may be, must be appreciated.

Your Quick Workbook: Self-Confidence Clinic

1. Are you currently struggling with self-confidence? What are the signs? (Signs: constant self-criticism, low self-esteem, negative comparisons, pushover tendencies, etc.)

    _____

    _____

2. Harmful thought patterns I need to take note of: Unreasonable generalizations (e.g., "I failed at one thing so I'm a failure at everything," "You never do anything right," etc.)

    _____

    _____

    Harsh judgments (e g., "You're good for nothing!")

    _____

    _____

    Self-criticism (e.g., "You're too damn slow")

_____

_____

3. Harmful behaviors I need to take note of (e.g., telling hurtful jokes about myself, letting opportunities pass me by, feeling limp when it's time to act, etc.):

_____

_____

CHAPTER FIVE

"Therefore do not worry about tomorrow, for tomorrow will worry about itself. Each day has enough trouble of its own."

–Matthew 6:34

OVERCOME ANXIETY AND DEPRESSION

It's normal to have ups and downs, good days and bad days. Aside from being an adult, the teenage years are probably the most intense and unstable years for the typical human. Feeling a little down sometimes goes with the territory. So does feeling a bit anxious.

But there's something else. Something that *shouldn't* go with the territory, but does. It's not exclusive to teenagers, but boy, are its effects on teenagers potentially life-defining. You know what it is?

It's a coin.

No, I'm not kidding you.

Anxiety and depression are like two sides of a coin. One rarely ever happens without the other. To be able to live free of these evil twins, you must understand them and take them out one by one.

Let's understand and deal with anxiety

I remember the first job interview I ever went for. Based on the requirements for the role, I knew I was more than qualified. But that didn't stop me from being anxious about the interview. I wondered if I had the right clothes to wear. I wondered if I'd wake up early enough to be able to prepare myself. I wondered if I'd get the job. I needed the job, but I didn't want to come across as desperate, even though I was very, very desperate. I don't think I slept a wink the night before.

As a result, I arrived at the interview with bags under my eyes and my clothes looking a bit rumpled. I remember feeling so stressed about the outcome of the interview, and I was just about to enter the interview room when the fact dawned on me that I was feeling so stressed about a job I hadn't even gotten. Needless to say, I completely messed up answers to the questions I was asked. My heart hammered against my ribs as I continually stammered and the interviewer eventually told me to have a nice day.

Miraculously, I got shortlisted for the role and had to take an aptitude test to proceed. Here's the contrast; the day I went for the aptitude test, I was completely relaxed about the outcome of the test because I had realized something: being *that* anxious wasn't going to help me.

This is the message I want to pass across to you. Feeling anxious is pretty normal, except when it starts to become a hindrance to your functioning.

We'll be discussing a bit more about anxiety in the next part.

Understanding anxiety: What is anxiety?

Anxiety is a combination of negative thoughts and feelings that result in intense worrying about something. This usually happens when you're facing a situation in which you have little to no control over the outcome. Ordinarily, a little anxiety can even be good for you, as it helps to keep you on your toes. But the moment anxiety becomes so intense that it starts interfering with your normal life, that's your cue that there's a problem.

Anxiety comes in many forms, and these forms are called anxiety disorders. From the name, I'm guessing you know what these disorders are about. Below are examples of some of them.

Generalized anxiety disorder

This type of anxiety disorder involves worrying excessively about ordinary, everyday life issues. A person suffering from GAD might feel a level of worry that is clearly out of proportion to the situation; for example, they may feel extremely anxious about the homework they have to do, an awkward conversation with a friend, etc. The worry felt by a person who suffers from generalized anxiety disorder is very difficult to control and can quickly feel overwhelming.

Panic attacks

Panic attacks are one of the most vicious types of anxiety disorders. Most people who suffer from panic attacks spend a lot of time worrying and anticipating the next panic attack. I once had a teen who told me a panic attack was like a heart attack. I asked her how she came to such a conclusion, and she told me she asked her grandma, who had suffered a heart attack, how it felt, and compared it with how she felt when she had panic attacks.

This goes to show just how serious panic attacks are, although they are not physically dangerous. Panic attacks are usually brought about by certain triggers, and it's not uncommon to feel chest pains and heart palpitations. They usually occur suddenly, and they feature probably the most intense and overwhelming feelings of all anxiety disorders.

Phobias

Phobias are a very specialized form of anxiety disorder involving very intense fears of particular objects or situations. For instance, I had a college friend who hated seeing a pattern of holes in any form. That phobia is called trypophobia. With phobias, the level of anxiety suffered usually doesn't match the situation.

Just like most anxiety disorders, people who suffer from one phobia or another usually spend a lot of time avoiding situations that will bring them face to face with their fears. That's why it's cruel to play pranks on people by exploiting something you know they fear. You never know what their response may be, as some people have panic attacks when put in a situation where they have to face their phobia.

Below are some examples of common phobias:

Fear of spiders: arachnophobia

Fear of closed spaces: claustrophobia

Fear of being embarrassed: catagelophobia

Fear of heights: acrophobia

Fear of flying: aerophobia

Fear of water: hydrophobia

Understanding anxiety: What are the signs?

There are some telltale signs of anxiety, and some of them are listed below:

- Feeling nervous or tense
- Hyperventilation
- Perspiration
- Racing heart
- Trembling
- Feeling weak or tired
- Trouble concentrating

Understanding anxiety: What are the effects?

Though anxiety is primarily a mental health issue, it has very extensive effects on the whole body. The reason for this is very simple; anxiety is the body's response to stressful situations, and once the stressful situation has been resolved, anxiety is supposed to subside.

In cases where there are anxiety disorders, however, the body remains in a state of alertness, ready to use the fight-or-flight response at all times. This is clearly not an ideal situation, and it has serious effects on the physical health of the person going forward.

Some of its effects are explained briefly below.

Breathing: It is not uncommon to hyperventilate when suffering from an anxiety disorder. Constant hyperventilation may lead to gasping for air, dizziness, a general feeling of fogginess that makes it difficult to concentrate, etc.

The heart and blood circulation: Long-term anxiety issues may predispose sufferers to the risk of heart failure.

Immune system: Over time, anxiety attacks drop the effectiveness of the immune system because of the hormones released into your body during bouts of anxiety.

One such hormone is cortisol. It prevents the release of infection-fighting antibodies, thereby lowering the ability of the body to fight infections effectively.

This is why chronic sufferers of anxiety attacks may come down easily with the flu, common cold, etc.

Other long-term effects of anxiety include insomnia, overthinking, substance use, depression, and harmful thoughts.

How to deal with anxiety once and for all

Living free of anxiety is the dream for many teenagers. Most of them just want to be able to live life normally without worrying about avoiding certain situations and triggers.

Maybe you're also like that. Maybe your biggest dream for now is to be able to live an anxiety-free life. Now, you might not think that it's possible. That's completely understandable. But this book wouldn't be complete if I didn't show you how you can in fact deal with anxiety once and for all.

Let me explain this a bit. Dealing with anxiety once and for all ***doesn't mean*** the absence of anxiety or anxiety-inducing situations. What it ***does mean*** is equipping yourself with the knowledge and tools to effectively combat every appearance of anxiety.

Ready to learn those tools?

Then let's dive right in.

1. Declutter

I know there's a whole chapter on this in this book, but this tool is so cool I had to talk about it here. Whether you're doing physical decluttering or mental decluttering, this principle is the same; decluttering helps you win back space that can be used to do productive things.

A word of caution: Ever heard of the phrase "nature abhors a vacuum"? Well, this principle is why every inch of physical or mental space you win by decluttering must be put into doing something productive intentionally. You have to be intentional about keeping your mental and physical space clutter-free, or the clutter is just going to come right back.

Enough spoilers.

2. Sleep early

Did I hear you say "What?!" I know you're not a kid anymore, but there's something you must understand: there are few, if any, stronger enablers of anxiety than sleep deprivation.

If you don't get enough sleep, you're basically giving anxiety a leg-up against you. This is because with a lack of sleep comes stress, and with stress comes cortisol. And with cortisol comes a fondness for the fight-or-flight response. And I'm sure you know the rest of the story.

So put your phone away and get some quality sleep.

3. Understand that feelings don't equal facts

Just because you feel stupid, doesn't mean you are stupid. Easier said than done, I know. But I never promised it was easy; I only promised it was possible.

I mentioned earlier in this book that most negative thinking patterns are not true. You must know this and use it as a weapon against negative thoughts. Here's what I personally do; I totally believe that negative thoughts are rarely ever true, so *every time* I realize negative thoughts are pulling me down, my first point of call is to tell myself,

"That's not true." From this point I then look for evidence against the negative thinking pattern.

Works like a charm, but it does take practice.

4. Practice gratitude religiously

Contrary to what you may think, gratitude is not one of those Zen things. It's a simple universal principle that, when used well, has the ability to extinguish anxious thoughts from your mind in a way that would make firefighters proud.

Again, I have a simple practice for this. Remember these two facts: there's always someone who has it worse than you do, and there's always something to be grateful for. I've had life get so rough for me in the past that the only thing I could think to be grateful for was the fact that I was still breathing. But it worked, and I'm in a much better place now.

Now for the "religiously" part. Create a system of gratitude whereby every week, you have time alone for the sole purpose of finding things in your life you're grateful for. Stick to that system for 60 days, and if it doesn't change your life, then I'll send you a coupon for a year's worth of any food you want.

(Only condition is that you have to actually eat that food every day for 365 days. Great deal, huh?)

Daily exercises to practice dealing with anxiety

Dealing with anxiety, especially if you suffer from an anxiety disorder, is something that has to be worked on daily. To make use of the exercises explained below, find a quiet place to practice each day.

Over time, you'll get much better at combatting anxiety, and this will boost your self-esteem also.

1. Counting

During anxiety attacks, everything often seems to happen in double-quick time, so practicing how to slow things down is wise. A great way to do this is by counting numbers in your mind. Usually, counting to 10 works very quickly to calm you down, but feel free to count to a higher number if you need to. Just ensure you set a target mentally before you start, then count till you reach the target. If the symptoms of anxiety don't subside, start all over again.

If it takes a bit of time, be patient and focus only on the counting.

2. Mindfulness

Being present in the moment is something that seems simple to do but is actually pretty tricky. Mindfulness requires you to stay in the moment without any form of judgment.

To practice this, find a quiet and comfortable place. You can take a cold cup of water or a hot cup of tea along with you. You don't necessarily have to drink it; the point of taking it is to notice how it feels in your hands. Touch is a very good way to shift your awareness away from your surroundings to yourself and back again. Do this multiple times till the anxiety subsides.

3. Physical exercise

Feel free to get creative with this. If you're a running person, run. If you're a gym buff, then have at it. The point is for you to do something physically engaging that you enjoy doing. This will promote the secretion of oxytocin and dopamine. These hormones promote relaxation and reduce stress and anxiety.

Understanding depression: What is depression?

Depression, or major depressive disorder if we're being technical, is a serious mental health condition where you lose interest in living and also suffer from being in a state of constant sadness. Depression makes it a lot harder to manage parts of normal life, and it is not unusual to want to sleep in and avoid everyone and everything as a result.

Unhappiness is not the same thing as depression. A lack of satisfaction or fulfillment is also not the same thing. Heck, boredom is not the same thing. Being unhappy or bored is a normal part of life. Not getting what you want out of life is also part of life, but it's not the same as depression. The major factor that differentiates depression from merely feeling sad is the nature and the duration of the sadness.

Just like feeling stressed and anxious for a prolonged period of time most likely indicates some form of anxiety disorder, feeling sad and unhappy constantly for a prolonged period of time might indicate a possibility of depression.

Clinically, a depression diagnosis is not possible unless you are experiencing five or more symptoms of the eight clinical depression criteria set forth by the DSM-5, and one of the symptoms must be either a depressed mood or a loss of pleasure. (The DSM-5 is the Diagnostic and Statistical Manual of Mental Health Disorders, 5th edition).

Below are the clinical symptoms of depression from Truschel (2022):

- Depressed mood most of the day, nearly every day

- Markedly diminished interest or pleasure in all, or almost all, activities most of the day, nearly every day

- Significant weight loss when not dieting or weight gain, or decrease or increase in appetite nearly every day

- A slowing down of thought and a reduction of physical movement (observable by others, not merely subjective feelings of restlessness or being slowed down)

- Fatigue or loss of energy nearly every day

- Feelings of worthlessness or excessive or inappropriate guilt nearly every day

- Diminished ability to think or concentrate, or indecisiveness, nearly every day

- Recurrent thoughts of death

Understanding depression: What are the signs?

Some signs of depression are easy to pinpoint, but others are not. Either way, below are some signs that point to a possibility of depression. Note that it is possible to be depressed without knowing it. This is why it's important for you to know the signs to look out for.

- **Drastic changes in eating**: This can be eating too much or too little.

- **Change in sleeping habits**: This can be sleeping too much or too little.

- **Alcohol and/or substance use**: Most people suffering from depression use these to help themselves cope.

- **Hyper positivity**: Perhaps surprisingly, you can be depressed and yet be the life of the party. Happiness/positivity in this case is used as a mask and not a genuine feeling.

- **Excessive fatigue**: This ties in with the tendency to lose interest in everything.

- **Difficulty concentrating**: When you lose interest in everything, it's not far-fetched to say that concentrating on stuff you're not even interested in would be difficult.

Understanding depression: What are the effects?

Just like anxiety disorders, depression affects the whole body, and its effects are very well known. Below are a few of them:

- **Insomnia**: If you suffer from depression, sleep deprivation is very common.

- **Heart disease**: A depressed person is not going to do much. Leading a sedentary lifestyle with little movement is a surefire way to predispose yourself to future cardiovascular problems.

- **Weight gain/loss**: A person who isn't eating properly or is eating too much will inevitably see the result in their body weight. Obesity is a real issue if you tilt to the weight gain side of the scale, while malnutrition is a possibility if you tilt to the weight loss side.

- **Sadness**: A perpetually sad person is like a pressure cooker; one day the pressure is going to get too much and the person is going to snap. This for me is the ultimate effect of depression on the body.

How to deal with depression once and for all

Personally, I wish there was a switch you could just flick off to make depression go away. But I know it doesn't work like that. Getting out of depression is serious business, and can only be achieved if you have the right information and support. Dealing with it once and for all will only work if you have the tools necessary to take on depression and win.

Some of these tools are explained briefly below:

1. Talk

Depression thrives best in isolation, where it can pulverize you with negative thoughts incessantly. As a way of relieving the pressure of having negative thought patterns constantly roaming in your mind, find someone you trust to talk to.

It will help you feel heard and understood, and will do wonders for your sense of belonging. If you can't find anyone you can speak to, I've got another idea for you (see #2).

2. Talk… with your creative gifts

I have personally never met anyone without any creative ability. Granted, I've not met even 1% of the human population, but it doesn't mean my assumption is wrong. In the event that you can't find someone you trust and can confide in, you can use your creative gifts as an outlet for how you feel.

If you're an artist, you can create art that represents how you feel. If you're a writer, you can pen down your thoughts. If you're a singer or play a musical instrument, you can write or play songs that express your innermost emotions. The point of doing this is to express yourself and diffuse the pressure that negative thinking patterns bring.

Speaking of negative thinking patterns…

3. Challenge negative thinking patterns

Like I said earlier when discussing anxiety, I operate with a cardinal belief when it comes to negative thoughts: they are never right. As a teenager, an overthinker, and a sufferer of depression, the odds are stacked against you. But you can bring them down several notches by challenging the negative thinking patterns that power a lot of the lies that make you miserable.

Start by applying the fact that your negative thoughts are not true. Once you know this and believe it, you'll find that you'll naturally start to look for evidence against your negative thoughts. Once you're able to start doing this with regularity, the seemingly ever-present mist of depression will begin receding, and you'll start to feel a lot better.

Daily exercises to practice dealing with depression

1. Create one rewarding goal per day

Obviously, this should not be a big goal or something that will take a ton of effort to achieve. It should be something simple and very encouraging, and something that you'd enjoy doing, even if your enjoyment of it is small. For instance, you can set a goal to read a chapter of a good book every day if that's your thing.

The point of setting this goal is to help you feel a sense of achievement by doing something you will likely derive pleasure from.

2. Create a routine and follow it

Depression strips structure from your life, so it is important to get some structure working for you. A gentle morning routine that has you completing easy tasks will work wonders for your confidence, satisfaction, and feeling of achievement.

3. Go for a run… or a walk… or a swim… just exercise

The benefits of exercise are well known. If you're suffering from depression, exercise is a great way to not only get back in shape, but also help boost your feelings of achievement.

Remember, the key is to do something you will derive pleasure from. So if you're like me and love taking walks, then do that. You don't necessarily have to go to the gym to exercise.

Wrapping up

Now that we have a thorough understanding of anxiety and depression, it is important to note that overcoming them is not a one-day job.

You must commit to practicing the systems and structures explained in this chapter to combat them so that your ultimate aim of living free of anxiety and depression can be achieved.

Your Quick Workbook: Getting Over Anxiety and Depression

1. My anxiety triggers

_____

_____

2. 1-week Gratitude Challenge

Today	What I'm grateful for
Sunday	
Monday	
Tuesday	
Wednesday	
Thursday	
Friday	
Saturday	

CHAPTER SIX

"May the God of hope fill you with all joy and peace in believing, so that by the power of the Holy Spirit you may abound in hope."

—Romans 15:13 -

THE ART OF DECLUTTERING

Come now! Let's dust the cobwebs and let in some air!

Have you ever watched "Hoarders," that show about people who compulsively hold on to all kinds of stuff? I have to admit that after watching an episode of that show, I have to fight the urge to toss out half of my stuff, even though I can also relate to that urge to keep stuff.

The truth: watching that show can make you want to dash out of your own living room and reach for the nearest wall where you can hit your head. It has become such an addictive show for me despite the fact that I hate what I see. But maybe now that I think about it, I'm not just addicted for nothing. That show is a constant reminder for me to take continuous stock of the things in my life and the people who make up my relationships, with a single brutal goal: **throw out the trash!**

In particular, the episode that nearly traumatized me (to put it lightly)—and I'm sure there are lots more that could do so—was about this lady that filled her home with stuff she found from dumpsters. She wouldn't stop. She kept picking things out and bringing them home. Her behavior got so bad that she had a maggot infestation. Of course it was gross! But still she wouldn't let go. Whaaaat!?!

But the thing that stands out for me whenever I watch the show is how the people who hoard stuff are often unaware of the negative effects their stash has on them. The lack of awareness about both the grossness and the danger of their behavior is what totally bewilders me every time I catch this show.

The fact that the hoarded stuff keeps accumulating and taking up space that's meant for other things is the real danger. Gosh! Think about the financial cost of some of those useless items that people actually buy and put in their homes just to fill the space. The horror!

So the people who hoard this stuff don't know exactly how much of a mess they're in because they don't consider the situation objectively. I can talk this way because I see that whatever they're hoarding is useless. They don't see that. When help arrives for them, they are first helped to see their hoard from an objective point of view, and this helps them out eventually.

What does it mean to declutter your mind?

The thing to note about the stuff that people hoard is that it isn't particularly useful to its owner. In fact, half the time, this junk is flat-out useless to anyone. Even if we could argue that some of the items might be useful, we certainly don't need such large amounts, no matter what they may be. In everything, moderation is very important.

Decluttering means removing unnecessary stuff from a place that is untidy or simply overcrowded. Points to note here are:

- The stuff being decluttered isn't necessary. If they were important, we would most definitely not be getting rid of them.

- The place we're moving them out of is overcrowded. That place isn't able to function anymore simply because it lacks space. So removing some items means that it'll function the way it's meant to.

When I was a kid, I actually looked forward to spring cleaning. Don't get it twisted, I hated being forced to clean when I could be doing other fun stuff, but I loved the fact that at some point during the process, I'd get to rediscover some of my old toys and treasures, play with them, and then pack them up carefully to be shipped to another kid who needed them but couldn't afford them. I also liked how fresh and revived the house always seemed afterward.

Decluttering your mind is much like decluttering your physical space in spring. I wasn't surprised to discover that decluttering your mind and decluttering your physical space are connected. Mental decluttering means taking a pause from whatever is going on in your head, checking in with yourself, and evaluating yourself mentally. It means making your mental health a priority.

Have you ever felt like there's no space in your head because so many things are going on in your mind? Thoughts of past events, processing feelings about the events, processing feelings about the people that were involved in the events, worrying about present events, freaking out majorly about the future, and trying to remember to stay hydrated through it all.

If that's you or that sounds remotely similar to anything you've experienced, I see you've met my old friend, Mental Clutter. You know the way your room suddenly becomes overtaken with knick-knacks, clothes, or other trivial items in the blink of an eye and suddenly there's no space to sit anywhere?

Yep.

In the same way, your mind can accumulate thoughts, worries, and other things that take up space and prevent it from functioning optimally. This mental clutter creeps in silently and overtakes the space you're meant to use for the important stuff. Kind of like cancer.

Decluttering may sound as tedious as a massive cleaning, and this might make you feel reluctant to get into it at all because it sounds like a lot of work. Well, the truth is that decluttering is in fact not a tedious process at all. It's great for your mental health, and the best part is that you begin to feel the benefits of decluttering your mind almost immediately.

It helps to improve your mood instantly, relieve stress, and focus better. It's great for improving your self-control, too. Best of all, it costs $0. Yay!

Mental decluttering is one of my favorite practices and I often recommend it to anyone who will listen. And sometimes to a couple of people who won't listen. What can I say? I'm a believer.

Signs that your mind is jam-packed

Imagine you're at the supermarket and rolling your cart along, picking up what you need. You walk up and down all the aisles, shopping for only the essentials. You find yourself eyeing some stuff on the shelves you'd like, but your budget demands you stick to what's on your list. Soon your cart is full and you're about to check out; then you hear the voice on the PA announce that there's a 3-minute window of opportunity to get whatever your cart can carry for free.

What would you do? Would you toss out all the basic stuff in your cart (that you can buy later) and rush to grab the stuff you really want that's probably worth hundreds of dollars?

Or would you miss out on the chance of a lifetime simply because your cart was already full? Me, I'd turn that cart over to empty it, race through the aisles, and pick up every one of those things I'd always wanted but couldn't afford.

That's kind of how decluttering works. Empty out stuff so the real gold and silver can come in. I've done this a lot. I still do it periodically because it's never a one-time thing. In fact, I'm itching to tell you about how I've successfully decluttered my relationships too. These things are exciting to discuss. The process may be hard, but when you start reaping the benefits, you'll want to shout it out and invite more people to join the train.

You might think that a mental declutter isn't right for you, but if you keep reading, you might find one or two reasons to reconsider. The following list contains a few telltale signs that you need to do a mental declutter.

You're finding it difficult to focus

Sometimes, when I'm working on projects (like writing this book, for example), I have days where I do my best work flawlessly and I hit a lot of goals without breaking a sweat. Then I have other days where getting through a chapter seems like a herculean task. Whenever I feel that way, I know I'm due for a "deep cleaning" or mental decluttering. The best part is that it works—every time. No kidding.

If you're finding it hard to focus on your important tasks or it takes a longer time than usual to get stuff done, you are definitely due for decluttering.

You're tired all the time

Do you find yourself thinking about how tired you are all the time? You might even be getting enough sleep, but as soon as you try to get some work done or even try to focus on your day-to-day activities, you start feeling mentally tired.

You might not be able to sleep well because your mind refuses to shut down. You might wake up feeling tired. These are clear signs of mental fatigue—a constantly working mind that won't rest. Having thoughts running through your mind all day is like leaving your laptop running at full speed every day; the laptop will start glitching more and more due to being overworked. That's exactly how your brain feels when you have all that mental clutter hanging around.

You're not as creative as you used to be

If you play an instrument or write poems, for example, you might have days where you just don't feel up to writing a new piece or playing a new song. That is a huge indicator that you need a good old-fashioned mental spring cleaning. The interesting part is that you don't particularly need to be a conventional creative (like an artist or musician) to notice your creativity dwindling. You might notice that you miss the obvious things or that it takes longer than usual for you to solve problems.

You're stuck doing unimportant things

Each day, we have a pretty good idea of the most important tasks we need to do to achieve our goals. Most productivity gurus will advise you to do the tasks that get you closer to your goals first thing or as soon as possible during the course of the day. If you find yourself focusing more on unimportant tasks or avoiding the important ones, it might be a sign that you have some issues to clarify.

A big element of procrastination has to do with having too much mental clutter. If you're not able to get clear on your goals and why you need them achieved, you may not be mentally prepared to do the work required.

Decluttering will help you refine your goals and master the steps you need to achieve them.

You can't seem to make up your mind

Someone once said that the risk that comes with making the wrong choice is nothing compared to the terror of being indecisive. I tend to agree with that quote because while taking your time to make up your mind may seem like a good idea on the surface, it might be an indication that your mind is too stressed to process information properly because of the mental junk. A mental decluttering might be very much in order.

You can't carry out your plans

It's easy to get stuck in that zone where you're not really achieving your plans but instead just moving along with life and letting things happen to you. You might wake up one day and realize that years have passed and you're not any closer to your goals. You might find yourself second-guessing decisions you've already made and overthinking things. Sometimes this is normal, but if it gets to the point where it's hindering you from actually moving forward, you need to do a declutter.

Now, decluttering your mind may not be the entire solution to the problem, but it's definitely a great way to start.

The bottom line here is that mental decluttering is essential for everyone—including you. It's a simple technique, but it's super effective with great benefits!

General benefits of mental decluttering

I guess it's time to talk about Vivian (not her real name). Vivian was one of the teenagers referred to a therapist because she had problems sleeping at night and had started failing a lot of classes. She was worried because she needed perfect grades for college and she didn't want to depend on sleeping pills any longer.

The first time Vivian walked into the office, she was pale and had dark circles under her eyes. After some sessions, she revealed that her parents had gone through a messy separation the previous summer (jeez, the increased number of divorces really does a number on teens). Even though she seemed fine with it at first, it turned out that she had repressed her emotions and tried to pretend everything was good. She had started overthinking, and it seemed like her mind was always working overtime. She tried to distract herself with various activities during the day, but at night she couldn't hide from it anymore.

They started off with mental decluttering, and after a couple of deep dive sessions, she said she felt so much better and was able to sleep well without the aid of sleeping pills. She was particularly excited when the therapist told her that the mental decluttering session was only the beginning.

Needless to say, as we they were rounding off their last sessions together, she looked brighter and more alert, especially without the dark circles under her eyes.

Now, I'm not by any means saying that clearing out the junk in your mind is the ultimate solution to all your problems. Rather, think of it as the "giant step" we take at the beginning of the solution. No matter which way the coin flip lands, it's always a win when you choose to clear your mind first.

The following are some benefits of decluttering your mind.

1. Decluttering relieves stress

Have you ever had a day where everything seemed to go terribly wrong? Probably started with a bad hair day, then forgetting to charge your phone, and ending dramatically with an allergic reaction to nuts that required a visit to the ER.

Your bad day may not be as dramatic as that, perhaps, but I've noticed that stress, like bad days, tends to worsen exponentially. It's kind of like stress attracting more stress, which ultimately leads to…you guessed right, even more stress.

Decluttering your mind is like ripping out the foundations from your tower of stress. All that stress comes crashing down.

Usually we tend to worry about events that get magnified because we obsess over them. When we examine the thoughts or ideas causing the stress under the lens of logic and self-compassion, we tend to see that we had no reason to worry in the first place, or at least not that much anyway.

The process of bringing out each thought, examining it objectively and deciding where it goes will help you to see what the fuss was about initially. Even if you don't end up solving the issue while decluttering mentally, you'll have a pretty good idea of how to solve it. I don't know about you, but that's a win in my book.

2. Decluttering helps you achieve self-control

How do you cope in those moments when the pressure mounts in your head and you feel like exploding?

I had to find a new way to get my emotions together. Mental decluttering was it for me. It was great! I could get my emotions under control anywhere. I simply needed to close my eyes for a few minutes. That was it. No need for long hikes to remote forest trails. Taking stock of and mentally rearranging your thoughts helps you to identify the root cause of your turbulent emotions and deal with it. Easy peasy.

3. Decluttering helps you to be self-compassionate

You might be familiar with the term "self-compassion." It's a pretty popular term, and it's probably one of my favorites. It simply means treating yourself the way you'd treat your best friend in the world—the way you'd give them a hug when they're feeling down or cut them some (or a lot of) slack when they mess up. Turned inward, that's self-compassion.

When you're down, you may find yourself engaging in negative self-talk and wanting to beat yourself up.

Taking the time to sort out your thoughts and remove unnecessarily negative ones will help you to slow down and assess yourself objectively. This self-reflection promotes gentleness and compassion for self.

I don't mean to sound like a broken record, but it really does work. The next time you're stuck mentally or you can't think of a solution to a problem, if there's some clutter in your environment or you have a messy room, try cleaning it up and putting away the unnecessary stuff. It sounds crazy, but you'll realize that you now have the mental space to think better after decluttering.

That's physical decluttering, and it has been shown to have lots of mental health benefits. How much more beneficial is mental decluttering? I'll let your results speak for themselves.

How decluttering helps with overthinking

Picture this: it's a sunny day and you're out in the park, trying to get some sun and just have a fun day in general. Now, imagine you're being followed around by someone screaming right in your ear with a trumpet. It's loud, it's uncomfortable, you can't focus, and every time you hear the trumpet, your eardrums rattle—only they don't sound like a rattle; they sound like doomsday mixed with frustration and intentional disregard.

So there's a couple of options here; you could get worried about the fact that something is ruining your special day, wonder why this is happening to you, blame yourself for letting this happen to you, and end up with a colossal headache, a ruined day, and tired eardrums (if you don't go deaf).

Or…

You could realize that being followed around by a trumpeter, no matter how enthusiastic, is seriously cramping your style. Having realized that, you could then try to ask the trumpet guy why he's following you and who sent him. If he gives you a clear answer as to who assigned him to bug you, you could politely ask the trumpeter to ask that person to stop, or even ask him directly to stop. If that option doesn't work out for you, you could ask the cops to arrest him and throw him out. Out of the park. Out of your life forever too. Et voila!

Which of these options would you prefer? Think a bit about your answer and why. I know it might be a no-brainer, but humor me; I'm getting somewhere with this.

Now that you know the option you'd prefer, which of these options do you actually practice? Do you just wander around with your head full of thoughts that keep running the same old track in your head, night after night and day after day? Or do you make an action plan and proceed to systematically eliminate the source of distraction and worry?

The awesome thing about being mentally tough and resilient is the fact that you can actually intentionally work on becoming mentally tough. It's like a muscle that you can train every day and watch grow. This means anyone and everyone can become mentally resilient. By the time you're done with this book, if you consistently practice the principles we've talked about here, you'll be shocked to find that your mental resilience will be developed to an appreciable extent.

I always say that overthinking rides on the shoulders of the past and the future. As much as you might be worried about your present situation, the major reason you tend to overthink is because you're worrying over what has happened in the past or fearing that whatever happened in your past will ruin your future. The present is neatly ignored, like that neglected present (ha, see what I did there?) from a distant aunt that sits under the Christmas tree month after month, till the dog probably mauls it.

The key to battling this tendency to overthink lies in your ability to challenge those thoughts, break the cycle, make peace with your past, be present in your present (last one, I promise), and anticipate your future with a smile on your face and hope in your heart.

When you do a mind declutter, every thought is categorically examined. You simply gather all the thoughts, worries, fears, and possibilities that your mind can imagine. Heads-up—it's a lot. Your mind is capable of producing these by the dozen.

The fun part is that when you keep examining each thought and tossing out these junk thoughts, you quickly realize they are mostly unfounded and you don't need to have so many of them around. Slowly but surely, your mind stops reeling in those worrisome thoughts and starts to go in the direction you point it at.

Sometimes when you're doing a mental spring cleaning, you don't even have to fully explore a thought right at that moment before you decide what to do with it. That's the great thing about this. You don't have to delve into any complicated thoughts or issues right at that very moment you're decluttering; you can just decide to revisit it later and file it in your mind as something to come back to.

Just that simple action of categorizing that worry, thought, or fear gives you some power over it, and you start to feel better almost immediately. Sure, you may not have solved that problem in its entirety, but you've **done something** about it, which your mind will see as a major win.

Is it possible that your mind has too many things to declutter? Are you afraid that you might not get everything out at once? No problem. You don't have to take care of everything at once. Depending on the time you have and other factors, you could either do a deep dive or lightly skim through your mind to get what you need just for that moment.

Some people might recommend doing a mental decluttering every once in a while when you really feel things coming to a head. I flat out disagree. I don't know about you, but I would hate to stay in a hotel where housekeeping only came to clean the room once a month or once in two months because they wanted the dirt to really pile up before they cleaned it up. Just think—the sheets, the toilets, all those things going unwashed? That's a huge **NO** for me. I expect that it wouldn't sit well with you either.

As far as I know and practice, you should do a mental decluttering every day. Specifically twice a day for starters, or even more than twice as you see fit. I don't like to make huge, showy promises, but I can guarantee that this works and very soon, you'll be able to guarantee it too.

How to declutter your mind right now

All right, let's get into it.

How would you clean a room? I imagine you might want to tidy the surfaces first, clear out all the litter, and put things back in their proper places. Then you might go ahead and wipe all the surfaces down, clear the cobwebs if any, and then vacuum all the dirt or sweep up all the dust. Good to go, right? Not quite.

Now that you've gotten your room clean, you need to plan a routine around *keeping* it clean. Once you've got that down, then you're home free.

We'll talk about a mental decluttering exercise you could do in 2 minutes in a bit. But first, let's take a look at some habits that can help you declutter your mind.

1. Talk to a trusted friend

Talking to someone you love and trust about what's going on in your head is a great way to sift through the mental maze that's your mind sometimes. It could be a face-to-face conversation, a text message, or a video call. You get to release any emotional tension, clear your head, and get your problems off your chest. This is especially perfect for you if you've been struggling to handle some issues on your own and you haven't been successful. If you don't feel encouraged to talk to a family member or friend about it, you could find a professional to talk to. Remember to always stay safe and go with your gut.

2. Consider keeping a journal

Journaling helps you to analyze your thoughts and organize your mind. The simple act of writing down whatever is going on in your head may seem small, but it has a lot of benefits. When your thoughts are on paper, your mind feels relaxed. Journaling also helps to reduce overthinking and negative thoughts, improves memory, and can even help you cope with depression. The greatest benefit of journaling, in my opinion, is the fact that it frees up your mind to focus on things that are more important than whatever mental clutter you had going on.

3 .Set your priorities straight

Oftentimes, things get muddled up in our heads—even more so when we overthink. You might begin to question your plans and ambitions. You might even start second-guessing yourself and feeling indecisive about your future plans. This will lead to you not actively working to achieve your goals but instead just passively going along with the flow.

Having your priorities figured out and visible is a great place to start whenever you get into a mental fog. Simply reevaluating your actions (or lack thereof) against the template of your goals and priorities can help you restore a semblance of order in your mental space.

4. Do a physical declutter

I talk a lot about clearing your mind, but it would be remiss of me to neglect the importance of physical order and its effect on your mental health. A tip I share all the time is that you should make clearing up your room or work desk one of the first things you do every day. This is because clearing up your space gives you a sense of accomplishment and is a great mood booster. It becomes easier for you to achieve your other goals when you've marked one goal off your to-do list first thing in the morning.

Also, the physical act of clearing up allows you to practice mindfulness, which is great for your mental health. Being aware of the present moment and being fully immersed in it helps you calm your brain and allows you to think clearly.

Let it go

Choosing not to hold on to negative emotions and past events that make you feel bad about yourself is a trusted way to free up mental space. Accepting that you're human and that humans make mistakes opens you up to self-compassion and less inner criticism. This lets you focus on your activities with all your brain power, which leads to better results.

Here's a simple exercise you can do to declutter your mind:

- Take note of your breathing pattern. Breathe in deeply, pause, and breathe out. Do this a couple of times. It helps to reduce your heart rate and blood pressure, clears your mind, and boosts your mood almost immediately.

- Write down everything that's on your mind. Feel free to be as descriptive as possible. It could be anything—for example, a list of things to do or a list of your emotions and why you feel that way.

Examples of things to do

- Get ready for my driving test
- Make dinner
- Text Aunt Elsa to congratulate her on the arrival of her new baby
- Do homework
- Visit the dentist

Examples of emotions you're feeling

- Sad because mom wouldn't listen when I tried to explain to her why I can't get groceries today
- Angry because my dog messed up my bed
- Anxious because there's a test tomorrow

- Scared because I don't know if I'll pass my driving test
- Blank because I have so much to do that I don't know where to begin

Work through your list. Sort out your tasks in order of importance if necessary. Sort out your emotions; observe them, identify their root cause, accept that your emotions do not define you, and let them go.

Finish off by repeating some positive affirmations that you enjoy or identify with.

That's it, folks! This won't take more than 5 or 10 minutes, and it is very effective.

Yes, you've got this!

As we wrap up this part of the book, I want you to know that you've got this. Whatever lack of confidence you felt should be knocked out using the principles we've discussed, because you deserve to feel confident and smart. You deserve to feel happy, free, and to enjoy every single day of your life. You can do this. Do it. Don't hesitate. Let's go to the final and shortest part of this book. It's going to be another enjoyable time, I promise.

Your Quick Workbook: Decluttering in Progress

1. Examples of thoughts that are making it hard for me to focus:

_____

_____

_____

2. People in my life that shouldn't be there:

_____

_____

_____

Personal decluttering progress tracker

Use the table below to give yourself a one-week challenge to declutter your thoughts. At the end of each day of the week, summarize your progress so far.

Day of the Week	My Progress Today
Sunday	
Monday	
Tuesday	
Wednesday	

Thursday	
Friday	
Saturday	

Part 3

Managing Your Mood and Stress Levels Without Sucking at It

There was a time when I thought that managing stress was all about going on vacation, sleeping in fancy hotel rooms, and going on boat rides. Now I know better.

No doubt, boat rides, golf, and nice hotel rooms can definitely help to take some stress off your shoulders, but there's a bit of a problem there. What if I can't afford a boat ride or pay to sleep in the presidential suite where there are mints on the pillows? Does that mean I'm sentenced to a life of stress?

The other problem is that no matter how wealthy your parents (or even you) are, you can't be on a boat ride every single day of your life. If, as a fast-growing teenager, you have to face some measure of stress daily, then it's wise to know exactly how to manage it daily too.

A vacation can help give you periodic relaxation and recuperation, but the everyday stress and mood booster is king. This final part of the book offers quality information on how to master your stress management without having to pay for hotel rooms (at least till you really can and want to pay for one), and how to keep your mood positive amidst all the challenges you might have to surmount on a daily basis as a teenager.

CHAPTER SEVEN

*"If you are tired from carrying heavy burdens, come to me
and I will give you rest. Take the yoke I give you. Put it on
your shoulders and learn from me. I am gentle and humble,
and you will find rest. This yoke is easy to bear, and this
burden is light."*

—Matthew 11:28-30

USING MINDFULNESS TO DEAL WITH OVERTHINKING AND TOXIC THOUGHTS

You probably wouldn't want to get mugged, right? So, to avoid getting mugged, you take safety precautions like getting home early and avoiding the dark, lonely places where you are most likely to be attacked. You might even try to predict what would happen if you were to get mugged and how to escape without getting hurt. Maybe even take self-defense classes.

Newsflash: Toxic thoughts are at least as dangerous as getting mugged. It's crazy how we take so many precautions to avoid danger to our physical bodies but get negligent with our mental and emotional health.

I want to make a sweeping declaration here; I'm not trying to scare you, I promise, but I'm speaking from a place of experience and this needs to be said.

Here it is: toxic thoughts can and WILL ruin your life. There. I said it. Now, calm down. I know your heart might be racing and you might even be freaking out. Just breathe. Relax. Yes, toxic thoughts are quite literally toxic, but they are very manageable.

You might be wondering, *So what? I tell myself the truth as I see it. What's the big deal? I definitely wouldn't lie to myself, and my inner voice couldn't possibly be wrong. I mean, I know myself best. Right?*

Wrong. First off, your inner voice is always going to be negative and critical about you—that's why it's called the inner critic. This means that you're actually not being as objective as you think. If the mirror of your self-perception has already been damaged by your inner voice, then the mirror you're looking into is not a clear reflection of reality at all.

Now here's the big deal. Toxic or negative thoughts have been shown to affect the physical as well the mental aspects of life. Not just that, but they have also been proven to have a lasting effect on the thinker.

The wild danger of toxic thoughts to your growth and self-esteem

I was intrigued to note the results of a study done in 2015 on a group of teenagers in Miami. The study discovered that teenagers who were not overweight but thought that they were overweight had a higher chance of being obese in the future. This meant that based on the mindset and thoughts they had about themselves, they started to develop an unhealthy diet and sedentary lifestyle that was compatible with obesity. At the end of the day, even though they were not overweight at first, they ended up becoming obese strictly as a product of the kind of thoughts they entertained about themselves. Crazy, right?

Does this mean that your thoughts actually have the power to direct your life? Those kids probably didn't want to be overweight (and they weren't), but because they thought that they were and accepted that they were, it became their reality.

I think we have no choice but to conclude here that thoughts DO have the power to direct our lives. Are you asking, *If thoughts have the power to direct my life, why isn't anything good happening to me even though I try to think of good things?*

Great question. The fact is, thinking positive thoughts will improve the quality of your life just like thinking negative ones will affect your life negatively. However, intentionality and consistency are key. Do you truly believe the positive thoughts or are you just trying out the idea so that you can condemn it? What are your systems for ensuring that you're applying this positive mindset to every facet of your life? What are your systems for making sure that you're thinking positively every day?

If you've read the book to this point, you should have a good idea of the answers to those questions. You'll still come across some juicy stuff in this chapter and the next. On we go!

Another study found that focusing on the negative aspect of an event led to lower self-esteem, a dissatisfaction with self, and psychological trauma which lasted as long as 8 weeks after the event. The more you focus on the negative in any situation, the more you're likely to keep seeing the negative in every other situation, and that ultimately affects how you interact with the world as well as with yourself.

Negative thinking has also been shown to cause high blood pressure even when you're not thinking negatively at a particular moment. It could also make you feel helpless when you're faced with stressful situations, which makes you unable to handle said situations and causes even more negative feelings and stressful situations.

I'll say it again. Toxic thoughts WILL ruin your life. Once you know this and you've accepted it, we can move on to combating them.

How mindfulness helps (real life benefits)

Have you ever caught yourself thinking something along the lines of *I didn't do X well; why am I such a failure?* or *They didn't smile at me when I said hello; they probably hate me.*

Sometimes we keep thinking about an event that happened in the past and we are worried that we might make the same mistake again. Other times we anticipate a future event that leaves us anxious and unable to concentrate on our present tasks.

Have you noticed that at least half the time, the sum of your worries is about a future or past event and hardly ever about the present? Don't get me wrong, we also end up worrying about our present, but that is largely overshadowed by our anxiety about the past and our worry for the future.

Now, this is where mindfulness comes in. Simply put, mindfulness is all about being aware of the present and regarding it in a neutral, non-judgmental manner. It means being present in this moment instead of worrying about the past or obsessing over the future.

The practice of mindfulness allows us to observe our thoughts as they come, prevents us from attaching too much importance to these thoughts, and also enables us to accept and let go of these thoughts without judgment or fear. It allows us to be objective and subsequently reduces our negative reactions to these thoughts.

One of the best ways to practice mindfulness is through meditation on the Bible. And that will give you success in spite of the challenges. God said, "This Book of the Law shall not depart from your mouth, but you[c] shall meditate in it day and night, that you may observe to do according to all that is written in it. For then you will make your way prosperous, and then you will have good success." —Joshua 1:8. Five minutes of daily meditation can go a long way.

Mindfulness means listening to our negative thoughts and saying, *These are just thoughts that I'm having. They do not represent my reality.* And it's true. These thoughts might be based on your reality in one way or another, but they do not actually represent your reality in any way.

Once you've acknowledged these thoughts from a safe, objective distance, you'll be better equipped to dismiss them altogether or to change the narrative. Either way, you'll notice that you're no longer attached to these thoughts or the proposed outcomes of them.

For example, instead of thinking, *I failed the last math test badly; that means I'll probably fail this one too and end up failing everything else and having to go to community college…*

Try thinking, *I'm having a thought about how I failed the last math test. I'm thinking that I'll end up failing the next one and not get into the college of my dreams. While this fear is understandable, I know it's not true because I've studied and had extra tutoring to help me pass this test. I'm positive that I'll do better this time.*

Did you note the difference between the two thought patterns? If you're thinking that it's not easy to transition from the first thought to the second thought in the example I just gave, it's okay—but let me tell you that it's easy. It gets easier with the practice of mindfulness, and as you do it more often, you'll find yourself naturally thinking more like the second example.

Mindfulness increases your self-esteem and self-confidence. A study carried out on students showed that the students who were taught to practice mindfulness had significantly higher self-esteem than the other group of students who were not taught about mindfulness. They found that mindfulness is a great way to increase self-esteem without focusing on positive achievements or other such factors. In other words, mindfulness is a more secure way to increase self-esteem (Peppington, 2013).

Another systematic review of the research on this topic also found that mindfulness training significantly improves self-esteem (Randall, 2015). Mindfulness helps you calm the hectic pace of your mind. You'll therefore be able to assess your thoughts, look at situations objectively and make better decisions. Better decisions lead to improved self-esteem and self-confidence. This will lead to a reduction in stress, anxiety, and negative emotions. The sweet life.

Mindfulness improves physical health as well. It's been shown to treat stress, reduce blood pressure, prevent heart disease, improve sleep, and do so much more (Jacobs et al., 2016).

It could also help with handling bullying and the depression that comes with bullying. Mindfulness techniques help children cope with the effects of bullying and can even prevent kids from becoming potential bullies (Zhou et al., 2017).

Academic success goes along nicely with decreased stress and anxiety because a student is able to better focus on their studies. Mindfulness practices have been directly linked with increased academic success in many studies of children, teens, and adults.

Welcome to the part where I advocate for mindfulness.

Mindfulness has a lot of benefits, and the exciting part is that you'll get to discover more personalized benefits when you start practicing it. There's really no way to go but up.

Learning to practice mindfulness

Some people think of mindfulness as stretching out for hours on end, contorting their bodies into fantastic positions. Mindfulness is all about you becoming aware of the present and all that it encompasses.

Now, how do you know if mindfulness is really what you need at this point? Good question. I personally believe that mindfulness practices are relevant to everyone, no matter their age, self-esteem level, self-confidence level, or mental/emotional maturity. Yep, everyone deserves to practice mindfulness.

Anyway, here are some signs that indicate that you'll greatly benefit from practicing mindfulness:

- You tend to overthink and focus on negative thoughts and feelings.
- You overeat or are always snacking.
- You notice that you're always feeling stressed, tense, or on edge.
- You struggle with depression, feelings of anxiety, and frequent panic attacks.
- You're not compassionate to yourself.

- You don't relate to friends and loved ones as well as you'd like.

The important thing to note is that practicing mindfulness should be a gentle, enjoyable process that should not induce stress, fear, or anxiety in you. It's a reminder of the happiness that exists in the here and now as opposed to the past or the future. It should be a source of joy and serenity, not stress or anxiety.

MINDFULNESS GUIDE FOR DEALING WITH OVERTHINKING

There are so many famous people who will forever be remembered because they were great or deep thinkers. They were scholars, poets, philosophers, and inventors. This is to say that thinking is a great thing—very important, even. Overthinking, however, isn't good no matter how minimal you think it is.

You might think being "a bit of an overthinker" helps you to achieve order and discipline in your life. You might even argue that it makes you a great planner. No, duh.

Every sportsman knows that sports teams and coaches spend a significant amount of time re-watching their games and even their competition's games to spot areas of weakness, see how they performed, and plan for future games. This is a very big part of sports and some might say that this habit has been directly responsible for winning lots of games. That's great. Necessary even. But the human mind doesn't need to work that way.

The big problem here is that overthinking crosses the line from normal functioning to getting stuck in a cycle where you're unable to let go of what someone said to you or how you felt about something that happened to you.

Your mind absorbs this negative feeling, dwells on it incessantly, and makes it the blueprint for future interactions which leads you to stress and overthink some more; on and on the cycle goes. Before you know it, an anxiety disorder might come along for the ride, and that makes things much more complicated. We've discussed this in detail in an earlier chapter.

Mindfulness is a very effective way to deal with overthinking. In fact, I daresay that mindfulness is the antithesis of overthinking. I like to think of it as a scene where overthinking runs kicking and screaming when it sees mindfulness enter the room. Mindfulness helps by drawing our attention from the future or the past into the present. Because overthinking avoids the present time, mindfulness is the perfect way to combat it.

Mindfulness focuses on self-compassion, acceptance, lack of judgment, and other positive thoughts. Overthinking dwells on negative emotions and tends to amplify them. If you catch yourself overthinking, a simple mindfulness exercise will allow you to experience positive emotions and overturn the negative emotions.

Mindfulness allows us to engage with negative thoughts in a non-judgmental atmosphere where we can examine each thought or feeling and let it pass without getting attached.

Being mindful also encourages you to pay attention to your body, which is most likely getting ignored right now because you're so focused on what's going on in your head. Simply listening to your heartbeat or your breath can help you stay mindful.

Refocusing your perspective is an effective way to deal with overthinking. Mindfulness helps to achieve this while also decluttering your mind. In essence, you'll be able to let go of the intrusive thoughts and achieve greater peace.

As your level of self-compassion increases, you'll begin to accept your mistakes and failures. You'll begin to accept that, as a human, you're prone to making mistakes. This will then increase your self-esteem and your self-confidence and help you to handle overthinking much better whenever it comes up.

The 4-7-8 technique

This is a pretty popular and effective exercise. It helps to relax you and increase your focus. Here are its simple steps:

- Find a comfortable, quiet position and settle yourself.

- Observe your breathing pattern for a few seconds.

- Breathe out through your mouth.

- Breathe in through your nose for 4 seconds and hold for 7 seconds.

- Breathe out through your mouth for 8 seconds.

- Repeat this for 5-7 minutes. No more than 7 minutes!

It might be difficult to achieve this breathing pattern at first, but consistent practice helps.

Your Quick Workbook: Mindfulness Self-acceptance

This exercise is focused on helping you get to know yourself a lot better and appreciate the things that are unique about you. Endeavor to answer these questions. It might be the first time you've ever thought about some of the answers, so take your time.

- Who am I?

_____

_____

- My typical best day:

_____

_____

- My favorite animal and why:

_____

_____

- Why my best friend is my best friend:

_____

_____

- Career I'd choose if there was zero hindrance:

_____

_____

- What makes me happy:

_____

_____

- What makes me sad:

_____

_____

CHAPTER EIGHT

"Be strong and courageous. Do not be afraid; do not be discouraged, for the LORD your God will be with you wherever you go."

—Joshua 1:9

MOOD MANAGER

Positive self-talk: The #1 mood booster

"The mind is like a parachute, it only works when it's open."

I still can't remember where I heard this quote, but it's been one of my favorites for years. I love it because it pretty much sums up the foundation for a healthy and happy mind and, by extension, a healthy and happy life.

There's something I've noticed from personal experience. Negative thoughts, anxiety, depression, and overthinking all tend to shut the mind in, walling it off and isolating it from the body, the environment, and other people. I have experienced this myself. A closed-off mind is like a dark cellar, blocked off by roots and overgrown vines. That might be an extreme example perhaps, but you get the point, right?

On the other hand, an open mind is full of light and is well ventilated and unafraid to interact with the body, its environment, other people, and even itself. It's open to learning and growing, abundant in grace and compassion for itself and others.

I don't know about you, but an open mind sounds very attractive to me. I can almost smell the sunlight and freshly washed linen scent that I associate with an open mind. Am I the only one who has these kinds of vivid imaginations? I hope not!

The big point here is that an open mind can quickly become a closed mind if not well maintained. We need to get in there, sweep up the dust and cobwebs, and get the window open.

I've always referred to positive self-talk as one of the easiest means of "maintaining" the mind. It means handing yourself some self-compassion, especially when things are tough and you're tempted to be tough on yourself as well. It means being your own cheerleader when the chips are down. It doesn't mean being oblivious to the realities of your situation, but you should approach the situation with a positive attitude in a productive manner.

Positive self-talk has tons of benefits. It increases your self-compassion, self-confidence, and self-esteem. It's an automatic mood booster and actually helps to reduce stress. It has been shown to increase your lifespan, make your immune system healthier, and give you greater life satisfaction overall.

Negative self-talk sounds like this: *If I tell them that I've changed my mind, everyone will be disappointed and probably hate me.*

Positive self-talk sounds like this: *Everyone knows that I have the right to change my mind. Anyone else could change theirs as well. They'll understand.*

Here are a few ways to practice positive self-talk and add it to your routine. Remember, practice makes perfect, and this is a gradual process, so don't be discouraged at the start but keep practicing.

- Speak positive affirmations.

Have positive affirmations that you connect with posted all around you on sticky notes or saved as your wallpaper on your devices. You can go a step further and set reminders to say these affirmations at regular intervals, especially when you feel you might have a stressful day ahead.

- Practice gratitude daily.

Simply recalling things you're grateful for at the beginning and end of each day really sets the tone for a positive day. You could also do a quick gratitude exercise when needed.

- Treat yourself like your best friend.

If your best friend was in a bad mood, what would you say to them to get them out of it? Try that for yourself.

- Be around positive people.

Some people are so positive and joyful that being around them alone is therapeutic. Spend more time with those kinds of people, especially if you're in a bad mood.

Identifying your mood and being real about how you feel

The terms "mood" and "emotion" are often used interchangeably. It's best to start by talking about the difference between them and how one can affect the other.

The word "emotion" encompasses a variety of experiences, but we can agree that your emotions are your feelings. Emotions also include your thoughts and thinking patterns as well as your urges and impulses. They are a normal part of human nature. They basically help us understand whatever we are experiencing and show us how to react to that experience.

Your mood is determined by your emotions. Figuring out what caused your mood and being honest about how you feel starts from understanding your emotions.

As you get older, you'll get a better handle on how you feel and even why you're feeling that way. That's emotional awareness. Knowing what you feel and why helps you decide which emotions you want and which ones you don't want.

Now, if you're reading this and thinking, *This sounds nothing like me*—relax. If you're not in touch with your emotions or you're not able to clearly define what you're feeling and why you're feeling that way, that's fine. Not everyone is naturally in touch with their emotions. Not everyone is naturally emotionally aware. The good part is that emotional awareness can be learned and improved on. Being emotionally aware means you're well on your way to having high emotional intelligence, which is a very useful life skill.

Emotions may feel like a big deal, but they come and go. They could be very intense, very mild, or average. However, there are bad ways of expressing them, which is probably why some emotions get a bad rap.

Of course, emotions aren't always negative. They can also be positive—like happiness, cheerfulness, gratefulness, or confidence. Regardless, all emotions are normal. They give us information about ourselves, no matter how bad they might make us feel. This means that avoiding negative emotions won't be helpful. Rather, accepting that we feel the way we feel is better. We don't have to obsess over these emotions or talk about them all the time, but we do have to acknowledge and accept them.

Further managing your mood

What do you do when you're in a bad mood? Do you lash out at others and spread the bad vibes? Do you withdraw into yourself and go incommunicado?

Are you the type of person who does everything possible to ignore your bad mood and your feelings? If you are, you're also more likely to spend time mindlessly scrolling through social media, binging Netflix, or attending parties you secretly dislike.

What if I told you that you could shake off your bad mood faster than you think? Or that you could manage your mood better? It may sound like a tall order, but I'm confident you can get to this point.

The first step is to identify your mood and try to find out what caused it. Take a moment to observe what you're thinking and feeling. Then try to think about why you feel that way. Saying these thoughts out loud might help provide some clarity. You could try saying, "I feel angry right now, but I also feel hurt because XYZ." Speaking to a trusted confidant may also provide better clarity. Doing something to break your thought patterns about that mood could help too. Taking a short walk or staring out your window may be all you need to reset.

The next step is to accept your emotions and, by extension, your mood. Give yourself some grace, no matter how you feel. Sure, you might be hurt by someone's act of betrayal and you might be annoyed with yourself for putting yourself in the position to get hurt in the first place. Those emotions are valid. But you also need to be understanding and compassionate towards yourself about the way you feel.

The next step is to let go of those feelings. After acknowledging your feelings, you don't have to stay attached to them. Make a conscious effort to let them go. The mindfulness practices we talked about earlier will help here.

Now, think of the proper mood you need to be in to make the best of your current situation. Be very precise about what you're trying to accomplish. Then put yourself in the right environment. For example, if you need to study but you're not in the mood, going to the library might help put you in the mood after you've examined your thoughts and followed the previous steps.

Hanging out with the right kind of people can help your feelings get to where they need to be. Sometimes, you don't have to even physically see the person or talk to them; merely thinking about them may be all you need. You could also try playing some music or doing calming exercises. Of course, positive self-talk is highly beneficial throughout this exercise.

Again, remember that practice makes perfect, so you need to give yourself grace and keep practicing. I'm rooting for you!

STRESS MANAGER

Identifying stressors

We talked a bit about stress earlier, but just to do a quick recap, stress is your body's response to a real or perceived threat. The stress hormones adrenaline and cortisol are released and they trigger the body's stress response, coordinated by the nervous system. This response was highly useful in the primitive era, but now our stress response gets triggered by events that aren't as dramatic as, say, being chased by a sabretooth tiger.

The more we have a stress response to events, the harder it becomes to shut down the response and the easier it is to trigger this response until you might find yourself stressing over everything thereafter as well.

Stressors are anything that causes a stress response. It could be an event, a place, a person, or even an emotion. Stressors could make you feel upset, anxious, tense, unable to focus, or unable to sleep.

Stress can affect you emotionally, physically, and mentally, or cause a change in your behavior. Emotional stress responses could include aggression, depression, or agitation. Physically, you could have a stomachache, headache, or upset stomach. Having aches and pains in other places could also be a sign of stress. A change in behavior, like altered sleeping or eating patterns, could be a result of stress too. If you notice yourself becoming suddenly careless or forgetful, you might be chronically stressed.

A very common stressor for many young people is school. It's not the easiest thing to stay afloat in school, pass tests and exams, avoid bullies, and still be cool. Peer pressure is also a good example of a common stressor. Struggling to keep up with grades while also trying to fit in could cause emotional stress and even change your behavioral patterns. And of course, traumatic events like witnessing a school shooting, a terrorist attack, or a natural disaster are potent stressors.

The big picture here is that anything that makes you feel uneasy or tense is a stressor. Thankfully, stress can be managed well. After you've identified your stressors, the next thing to do is to anticipate them and try to avoid them or plan ahead to manage them.

Anticipating stress

The Covid pandemic was a high-stress period for everyone, and truthfully, I doubt anyone could have anticipated the extent of the pandemic and how it affected us all. I'm sure one of the key regrets for most public health experts and advisors would be a lack of preparation for the pandemic. Tough.

Thankfully, we can anticipate most potentially stressful situations, and that'll help you to manage stress or even prevent it entirely. One way to anticipate stress is by planning ahead. If you've analyzed (but not *over*analyzed!) a possible stressor, you can prepare your mind by planning ahead and conditioning yourself to reduce your stress reaction.

You could also avoid the potentially stressful situation altogether, especially if you're not confident that you can handle that level of stress or that it's necessary to be in that situation in the first place.

Life-changing events, while positive, might be a source of stress for us. A simple way to manage this is to reduce the importance of that event. For example, tell yourself that winning this competition is good, but you've participated in similar competitions and won before, so this one isn't that big a deal. If your family and friends are watching, remind yourself that they'll love you no matter what.

Another cause of stress could be the uncertainty of the future. Not having the right information or the right perspective could cause anxiety. The best way to handle this is to ask for more information and get as many details as possible. This will help you reduce any stress you might feel or avoid it altogether.

Managing stress

A big part of stress management has to do with taking consistent action and building up good habits. As we mentioned in the previous section, being aware of your stressors and anticipating stressful situations is huge.

When you find yourself in a stressful situation, immediately try to identify the stressor. Then identify factors that you can control and those you can't. If you can control some factors, such as leaving the environment for a bit, then do so.

If the thought of doing something (having a difficult talk with a friend, for example) is stressing you, break down your steps into smaller chunks. You can send a text to that friend and set a time for a meeting. Before the meeting, prepare yourself and rehearse what to say. You may even want to take notes. Then, when you meet your friend, you can be honest about how you've been stressed about the meeting. They will likely be very understanding.

Sometimes all you can do is acknowledge the stressor, work through your feelings, accept that you are powerless to do something about the situation, and let it go.

One great habit that helps with managing stress is getting adequate sleep. Eight to ten hours of sleep per night is recommended. Having great sleep hygiene will promote restful sleep. This might mean taking a relaxing shower before bed, limiting your screen time at least an hour before bed, and thinking positive thoughts right before you go to sleep. It's important to only associate your bed with sleep, so don't stay in bed to do homework or have stressful conversations. Have a dedicated desk or table for schoolwork that's separate from your bed, if possible. This will help your body to associate your bed with relaxation and sleep.

Reducing caffeine intake or avoiding caffeine altogether can also be useful in managing stress. In general, keeping to a healthy diet is a great way to reduce stress. Avoid sugary, fatty, and junk food. Opt for healthier choices like salads, fruits, and lean proteins. Avoid drinking alcohol, avoid recreational drugs, and stay well hydrated. This sounds like the average spiel, but I promise that it contributes significantly to your ability to manage stress.

Again, avoiding negative self-talk and replacing it with positive self-talk in a mindful manner helps enormously with stress management. Dousing the flames of your inner turmoil with waves of self-compassion, self-acceptance, and self-confidence will help you to manage stress from the inside out. This technique is especially useful when you are not able to control the stressor. Practicing mindfulness wins, always.

More helpful exercises and activities

Sometimes you might experience stress that's fueled by intense emotions. In these situations, having a "bank" of good habits stored up may just work for you.

Here are some exercises you can practice in such situations.

Breathe.

A simple breathing exercise will help to empty your mind and calm your thoughts.

- Lie on your back comfortably and place your hands on your stomach with your fingers loosely linked.

- Inhale for 4 seconds. Watch as the breath fills your abdomen, your chest, and then your mouth. As your stomach expands, your fingers will be separated gently.

- Hold your breath for 7 seconds; stay focused on your body and breath.

- Exhale for 8 seconds, slowly.

- You'll observe that you start to feel relaxed after a few breaths. You can continue this for about 5 minutes.

Note that if you're already familiar with breathing exercises, you can do this while seated instead.

Relax.

- Your body can sense when your mind is ready to either fight or flee. Sometimes you might get an urge to stand and pace or do something that communicates how tense your body is.

- The key here is to consciously do the opposite of what your body wants to do.

- Consciously relax your body. Take a seat, still your shaking legs, and attempt to regulate your breathing.

- Slowly scan your body for areas of tension and consciously release the tension in those areas. You'll be surprised by how much better you feel.

Take a rain check.

Sometimes taking a mental vacation is the best way to deal with a stressful situation. Just close your eyes, take a few deep breaths and imagine yourself in a calm, happy place. Stepping back from the current situation temporarily won't hurt.

Journal.

Failure to deal with stressful situations or being exposed to several stressful situations consecutively might leave you dealing with many emotions that are all vying to be expressed. This will definitely increase your stress levels and emotional tension.

A perfect way to allow each emotion to be expressed in a way that makes it easier for you to deal with each of them properly is journaling.

Journaling provides a place for you to grow, question ideas, and explore concepts without judgment. It also helps you build healthy self-esteem and self-confidence. Managing stress through journaling is effective because it affords you the space to stop and reflect on your thoughts. Spending time reflecting on these things can help reduce mental strain and relieve stress.

Your self-knowledge is also improved when you journal. It's common to lead a busy life, from school to practice to club activities or volunteer meetings. Oftentimes, you might not have time to see if you even *want* to do all the things you're doing, or if you're only doing them as a result of pressure from your family or your peers.

Emotional tensions also can be released and processed through writing in your journal. Not even your grades are left out—journaling improves your writing skills, which is great for school.

Journaling can even help you solve problems because the creative side of your brain (the right side) is involved in the process, and this allows you to see things from a fresh perspective.

If you're confused about what to write in your journal, here are five prompts to get you started:

- How are you feeling right now?

- What are you worried about right now? List them all out.

- What are three positive things that happened to you or that you witnessed today? Dig deep. What are you grateful for?

- What's your inner critic saying about your decisions and actions? Write it all down. Challenge each thought lovingly and with grace.

- Write a love letter to yourself.

Remember that these are just guides; you can write whatever you feel like writing in your journal. Anything!

Do some physical exercise.

You probably know this already, but exercise helps the body produce more endorphins, which are the neurotransmitters that promote the feeling of wellbeing. Exercise relieves stress and is a great way to meditate if you're not fond of sitting still.

Activities you can try are walking, running, swimming, and so on. Do whatever you love.

Also, spend a considerable amount of time outside when you can. Many people talk about how therapeutic being in nature is, and I tend to agree. Make it a habit to take a walk every day (or preferably twice a day!) in your favorite park. This is not the same as walking to the mall with your friends. This is a time that should be reserved for mindfulness and an appreciation of nature. You may even listen to your favorite calming music while you do this.

Join a support group/Talk to a parent or trusted friend

Sometimes, you might not be able to stop the pattern of negative thoughts in your head. Or you could just feel like you have way too many feelings and you can't sort them out on your own. You may not even be able to effectively carry out some of the exercises in this book because you're feeling overwhelmed or simply don't know where to start.

Talking to someone is a great way to get out of your head and get the support you need. Make sure you talk to someone who you trust. If you don't feel safe talking to anyone around you, try joining a support group. You can search for support groups online and join in virtually or attend physical meetings.

Alternatively, if you don't like either of these options, you could speak to a therapist. The important thing is to get the support you need.

CHRISTIAN MINDFULNESS FOR TEENS

At this point, I want to emphasize the importance of mindfulness for teens from a Biblical perspective.

As a teenager, you might not always realize that you are in the most crucial season of your life, but believe me, this is the time to lay the foundation. By overthinking, you're continually sapping yourself of the energy that you need to navigate these times. In this section, and in addition to all that we've already discussed, I will give five pieces of advice:

1. Dream big

You don't yet know what you'll become in life—so think as BIG as possible. Don't limit your dreams to your environment; you're bigger than that. Don't permit any circumstances or person to put you down. Cultivate resilience and discipline. Think BIG no matter what! Be gracious to yourself. There is no limit to what you can become. God has a plan for your life.

A passage of Scripture you can always meditate upon to keep yourself in remembrance of this point is: *"For I know the plans I have for you," declares the Lord, "plans to prosper you and not to harm you, plans to give you hope and a future."*—Jeremiah 29:11.

2. Be happy every day

Yes! Be happy!

"A cheerful heart is a good medicine, but a crushed spirit dries up the bones."—Proverbs 17:22

3. Cultivate a positive mindset

Someone once said, "The world is a reflection of your mindset." If you think the world is against you, then that's what you'll get. If you think people love you, that's what you'll get too. Whatever you have in your mind is what you'll see in the world. That's logical, right?

If you have a negative mindset, people will perceive that and react negatively toward you. That's why we must feed our minds with positive thinking and words of faith to remain positive about life. You have to build your self-esteem. Know who you are. You are unique and different, so be positive and confident.

4. Boost your brain power

As I already mentioned in this book, make sure you're giving yourself enough time to sleep. Choose healthy foods. Avoid alcohol and drugs because many lives are destroyed by these substances.

If you don't believe me, consider these statistics: in the USA, more than 74,000 people died in 2021 as a result of alcohol or drugs (Centers for Disease Control and Prevention, 2022). My wife works at a hospital in New York, and she's told me that for more than 10 years, almost every week, she's had to see firsthand how drug abuse destroys the lives of so many young people.

Over 90% of adults who have an addiction began to drink alcohol or use drugs when they were teenagers (National Institute on Drug Abuse, 2021).

Remember, Jesus is the rescue line for your life. No matter how bad your life seems to be, He can restore it. God is bigger than all of your problems. No matter what challenges you're facing right now, He has a way out for you.

God loves you.

You were born for the better! You are loved, and God has a bright future for you! He wants to set you free to enjoy the fullness of life. So take care of your brain, take care of your mind, and take care of your body!

5. Never forget God has a great plan for you!

Yes, He has a dream for you.

Think of the story of Joseph. Joseph was a privileged child in his family. His father loved him more than his other siblings. Consequently, his brothers hated him. One day, they tried to kill him. They sold him as a slave into Egypt. Joseph was only about 17 years old at the time, and he remained a slave for almost 10 years. One day, after an incident, his master put him in jail. But God was with him and removed him from prison. Seemingly overnight, Joseph became the First Minister of Egypt right after the pharaoh (Genesis 37). God's dream for His child always prevails.

Never forget, God has a dream for you too. Follow His instructions. He has a destiny for you.

Let's look at a different example. David was less appreciated by his family; he was the youngest child, and his father put him in the field to take care of the sheep. There, he experienced both freezing and sweltering temperatures. One day, God sent a prophet to choose among the children of David's father the one who would become the next King of Israel. His father presented all his children to the prophet, but he forgot David. The prophet asked him if these were all his children, and only then did he remember David. David was finally brought in, and

God chose him as King of Israel. He was just a teenager, but God had a destiny for him. As a teenager, you may be in the wilderness right now, but God has a destiny for you as well (1 Samuel 16).

God also has a purpose for your life, as we can see through this third story. In about 606 BC, the country of Israel fell under the power of Babylon. Babylon (present-day Iraq) took many promising young people captive. Daniel, a teenager, was one of them. After a very long and humiliating trip from Israel to Babylon (more than 1,300 miles), Daniel arrived at Babylon. It was not easy for him to be in a new country without his parents, but God blessed him there, and he became one of the leaders of Babylon. Despite the challenges of his life, God had a purpose for Daniel. Think of this story and tell yourself to never give up. God has a purpose for your life (Daniel 1-6).

Finally, God has a special mission for your life on this Earth. Consider this story: In the Persian Empire, the Jews experienced a great deal of racism. A plot had been carefully laid out to eliminate all the Jews. It was a time of great panic. A young woman named Esther knew about the situation. She fasted and prayed to God about it; then she risked her life by telling the king about this plot. God answered her prayers. The Jews were delivered. Like He did with young Esther, God has a special mission for you on this Earth. Challenge yourself. Do not hesitate to take risks with God (Esther 3-7).

Do not waste your valuable time overthinking the challenges of your life. Be mindful! With Jesus, everything is possible.

Your Quick Workbook

1. Mood review

In the following exercise, think about how you tend to act when you're in different moods.

- When angry, I tend to:

_____

_____

- When sad, I tend to:

_____

_____

- When nervous, I tend to:

_____

_____

- When frustrated, I tend to:

_____

_____

- When anxious, I tend to:

_____

_____

2. Anticipating stressful situations

Stressful situations can be hard to deal with, but it becomes easier when you're able to anticipate them. This exercise helps you practice the art of anticipating stressful situations and learning that some things can be controlled and some can't. It's always best to avoid worrying about things you can't control and focus on what you can.

Situation	Factors I Can Control	Factors I Can't Control
Exams are coming up	Studying hard Resting adequately	Whether the exam will be postponed The teacher's mood on the

	Reviewing the material the day before Praying about the exam Waking up early the morning of the exam	morning of the exam The weather on the day of the exam
Mom and Dad fight nearly every evening		
I need to pass my driver's license test		
I'm preparing for a job interview		
I really want to win the game next week		

I need to get into college		

CONCLUSION

In the beginning of this book, I thoroughly explained my experience with overthinking and how I've seen many teenagers struggle with it. There's been a lot of talk about in terms of its symptoms and effects. I hope I've also assured you that you have the power to stop overthinking.

I've been about fulfilling my promise, teaching you all about boosting your self-confidence, decluttering your mind, understanding how to deal with negative thoughts, using mindfulness, and a lot of other effective methods for overcoming overthinking as a teenager.

If you've completed the many workbook sections and exercises, answered the prompts, and carefully read the thorough explanations offered in this book, I believe that you've gained some perspective and experienced a transformation in your thinking habits.

Remember, it's all about practicing every one of the principles we've gone over in this book, consistently. That's the only way this is going to bring you total freedom from this overthinking tendency that you're struggling with. Here's to you as you practice the exercises again and again, as you trust in God to help you through, and as you make these principles a part of your life.

Did you enjoy reading this book? Then you need to leave me a review! Please go to the Kindle store and do that for me. Thanks!

Thank You

Thank you so much for purchasing my book.

You could have picked any other book, but you chose this one.

So, THANK YOU for getting this book and for making it all the way to the end.

Before you go, I wanted to ask you for one small favor. **Could you please consider posting a review on Amazon? Posting a review is the best and easiest way to spread the information contained in this book.**

Your feedback will help me to write the kinds of books that will help you in your personal growth. It would mean a lot to me to hear from you.

Leave a review on Amazon US. SCAN with your camera

Leave a review on Amazon US. SCAN with your camera

REFERENCES

Centers for Disease Control and Prevention. (2022, March 18). Alcohol deaths on the rise and suicide declines. Retrieved from https://www.cdc.gov/nchs/pressroom/podcasts/2022/20220318/20220318.htm

Dyregrov, A., & Yule, W. (2006). A review of PTSD in children. *Child and Adolescent Mental Health*, *11*(4), 176–184.

Harris, O., Lawes, A., Andrews, C., & Jacobsen, P. (2021). Kintsugi—Identity change and reconstruction following an episode of psychosis: a systematic review and thematic synthesis. *Early Intervention in Psychiatry*, *16*(7).

Leonard, E. M., Salman, S., & Nurse, C. A. (2018). Sensory processing and integration at the carotid body tripartite synapse: neurotransmitter functions and effects of chronic hypoxia. *Frontiers in Physiology*, *9*(225), 225.

McKay, M. H., & Richard, R. (2022). Efficiency of algorithmic policing tools: a nod to CN Parkinson. *Canadian Artificial Intelligence Association*. Retrieved from

https://caiac.pubpub.org/pub/88z04l0t/release/1

National Institute on Drug Abuse. (2021). Principles of adolescent substance use disorder treatment: a research-based guide. Retrieved from https://nida.nih.gov/publications/principles-adolescent-substance-use-disorder-treatment-research-based-guide/introduction

Pepping, C., O'Donovan, A., & Davis, P. J. (2013). The positive effects of mindfulness on self-esteem. *The Journal of Positive Psychology, 8*(5), 376–386.

Randal, C., Pratt, D. & Bucci, S. (2015). Mindfulness and self-esteem: a systematic review. *Mindfulness, 6*(6), 1366–1378.

Sanghvi, S., & Nakhat, P. (2020). Sleep practices of iGen: the quantitative analysis along with suggestive techniques. *Journal of Psychosocial Research, 15*(2), 589–597.

Sutin, A. R., & Terracciano, A. (2015). Body weight misperception in adolescence and incident obesity in young adulthood. *Psychological Science, 26*(4), 507–511.

Truschel, J. (2022). Depression definition and DSM-5 diagnostic criteria. *Psycom.* Retrieved from https://www.psycom.net/depression/major-depressive-disorder/dsm-5-depression-criteria

University of South Florida. (n.d.). What is self-confidence? *Counseling Center.* Retrieved from https://www.usf.edu/student-affairs/counseling-center/top-concerns/what-is-self-confidence.aspx

Widick, C., Parker, C. A., & Knefelkamp, L. (1978). Erik Erikson and psychosocial development. *New Directions for Student Services, 1978*(4), 1–17.

Printed in Great Britain
by Amazon